PHIL SMITH

ON WALKING

...AND STALKING SEBALD

A GUIDE TO GOING BEYOND

WANDERING AROUND LOOKING AT STUFF

First published in 2014 by:
Triarchy Press
Station Offices, Axminster, Devon, EX13 5PF, UK

+44 (0)1297 631456
info@triarchypress.net
www.triarchypress.net

A catalogue record for this book is available from the British Library.

Paperback ISBN: 978-1-909470-30-9

I have ditched my aliases this time to pass on the secrets of my hyper-sensitised walking.

This is walking as art, hyper-strolling, taking the ramble on a ramble, revolutionary walking, pilgrimage, extreme walking and walking for a change.

The ideas and tactics here are ones that anyone can use; whether for a stroll around the corner or a pilgrimage to a shrine that has yet to be built. Take the friend in your head, the people you love and the strangers you encounter on the journeys of their lives. This is very far from the last word on walking, but it will be mine.

Phil Smith of 'Wrights & Sites'
(aka Crab Man, Mytho, Anton Vagus, Spacetart)
Author of *Mythogeography* and *Counter-Tourism.*

Contents

Who me?

MOST OF MY WALKS have been made in Europe, a few in Shanghai, many in South Devon in England; most of all I have walked in my own small city of Exeter. I am classified in official documentation as white, male, heterosexual, late middle-aged, mono-lingual and overweight; but all that can change... I am irrationally fearful of dogs. Where there was once a Midlands accent, now there is barely a trace.

This book is coloured by my geographical, cultural and personal experiences. If they seem remote, eccentric or painfully inhibited, then I have to leave it to you to rearrange the structures and principles here to get at the same, or much better, effects. Varying tastes may pose even greater challenges. For this 'great walk' is mostly about subjectivities, those individual cosmologies inside each one of us that are increasingly under assault from homogenised freedoms and fundamentalisms; besieged ruins from which we will now build the future, or not at all.

Whenever I use the word 'walking' in a general sense it is always intended to include wanders that involve the use of prostheses, mechanical limbs or wheelchairs; there is nothing here intended to idealise any one variation of the human body over any other, but to place each of our many kinds among that variegation which is the affordance of life.

Superstitions

DO THEM ALL — salute magpies, dance between the cracks in the pavement, walk carefully under ladders.

> *"Try not to die like a dog."*
> Ralph Richardson the tailor, handing Mick Travis
> a gold lamé suit, in the movie *O Lucky Man!* (1973)

Approximate translation:

> *"This is your chance to live like an angel."*

Invitation

I WOULD LIKE YOU to join me on a walk. It will take us along roads, through towns and villages, and across beaches and heaths that I have never visited before. We will be exploring as we go, heading off at tangents, and every now and then stopping for philosophical and tactical refreshments as we happen upon opportunities for them: techniques, stories and ideas. I'll be trying out different ways of subverting heritage sites, repeating the route of a well-known literary walk and looking for a grandfather. Of course, this is just one of the many walks that I have made and make, but they often seem to overlap with each other, so this is not just a walk, but a kind of walking that we will be doing together. Before we set off to East Anglia, just so you have some idea of what I am up to, I would like to tell you about...

What I do when I walk

BEFORE I BEGAN TO WALK, to walk in the way I do now, I had twenty years writing plays for the theatre. I did other things, of course – toured with shows, cleaned libraries, cut grass on council estates, taught in a prison, co-ordinated a community publishers, taught Symbolist Theatre to undergraduates, organised Peoples' Fairs and helped collect food for the families of striking South Wales miners – but mostly I wrote, co-wrote or devised plays (over a hundred of them).

It was a privileged profession and I am still involved. When it goes right (only ever thanks to collaborations with colleagues far more talented than me), well, it's hard to decently describe the intense experience of those special times: sitting in the middle of five hundred people who are responding to your dramaturgical caresses as you take them through the introductions, foreplays, revelations and climaxes of terrible returns, unforgivable surrenders and infatuations with monsters. When the to-and-fro between audience and stage, gesture followed by response, followed by look, followed by laughter, a gasp spreading across thirty rows of spectators, reaches a finale and the audience can be held (and this is only when it really works, right?) bursting to shout and cheer... and finally the flood is released. Wow.

By now around 3 million people have been to see the plays I have worked on. I have been to see them performed in theatres in Munich, Warsaw, Shanghai, Krakow and St Petersburg, in smart stadttheaters and in miners' welfare halls. I would have to be a miserable man to pretend I have not had a blessed and happy working life, and the rest of it has been pretty fab too; serial relationships finally blossoming into twenty years of togetherness and a daughter and son. Part of the fun has been living such a life that most of my friends have no idea what I have done. I rather like not being wholly known or understood. Any transitory heartbreak along these shadowy ways has been down to my own clumsiness. Major tragedies have mostly been avoided, though I will have to face some dark memories on my walk with you; we have sat with our children in ambulances and in hospital wards a few times, but somehow and so far we got away unscathed each time. I have often been angry at the injustices done to others, but I have never had anything to complain about on my own account; and even in the midst of some bitter and occasionally violent political struggles, with a couple of very scary moments along the way, there has always been the joy of comradeship in a shared endeavour (and we won a lot of the struggles too).

It may seem odd, then, that I see walking not as a retirement from political struggle or from the sensual pleasures of entertainment, but as a further intensifying of both.

When I walk I draw upon layers of understanding that I have had to gather together in order to shape performances or to make political arguments; I am sensitive to the ways that the land and the cities are managed, owned, controlled and exploited. I am sensitive to the flows of power: information, energy, deference. I am also aware of contradictions in these places; I look out for those pressures that can, unplanned, open up temporarily free spaces, holey spaces, hubs where uncontained overlaps or the torque of bearing down in one place tears open a useful hole in another: these are places where, until we can at last all be free, we might for a while find space to act as we wish...

I would not want to pretend that there is any one right way to walk. The walking I propose here strides along beside all sorts of other walkings: walking to fetch water, rambling and hiking, walking for health, the walk of hunters, the walk of a crab across the floor of a rockpool, the walk to work and school and shops, lovers walking hand in hand. Neither does the walking I present here take only one form. You are free to use the ideas and experiences here and turn them into whatever kind of walking you wish: romantic, subversive, nosey, convivial, meditational, whatever. I like multiplicity and I think there may be some good in it – so, as long as your walking does not exclude the walking of others, I will be chuffed to think you are using any tactics or ideas here. At the same time I am giving myself the same privilege in the pages that follow: to walk the walk I want to walk and to evangelise about its qualities.

Along the way I will find it hard not to be sensitive to emblems and symbols; I know how they are used by playwrights and I use that 'insider' knowledge to guess myself inside the codes and secret languages of those who seek to influence. I know the secret meanings of the logos of Shell, Tate & Lyle, Magnox and the Ordnance Survey and I wonder at the mindset of companies that appropriate images of spirituality and what exactly it might be that they are throwing down a gauntlet to. To nail my symbolic colours to the mast, I am against the broad arrow of government and for the creative breath of the Awen:

The first is a heraldic steal from the Sidney family coat of arms, used to represent the authority and ownership of the British state (that is why prisoners once had arrows on their uniforms, because their uniforms were state property). The second is a symbol that turns up (appears or reappears, according to your sympathies, I am happy with its meaning either way) during the nineteenth century 'Celtic Revival' as a representation of both creative inspiration and the 'breath' that brings the universe into being.

By walking I have not denied myself the physical pleasures of performance. However, there is a more humbling aspect to walking; for it is not the walker, but the terrain, natural and built, that mostly makes the walk. The walker takes a far more powerful and experienced lover than any audience. Sun, tropical storms, traffic, snow, mists; the terrain is not your backdrop, but seizes the action as its author and agonist. The city jabs you in both eyes with its yawning inequalities pushed so close together; a sensitive walk up any High Street is a Pilgrim's Progress.

It is not all injustices and passions, though. Even more intense for a walker can be a joy in the textures of things. I place my fingertips on an eroded red sandstone sculpture of a horse, a little of the stone comes away and in my palm I hold a 300-million-year-old desert. I run the back of my hand over a rusting name plaque and what I feel missing is the industry it once advertised; dropped so suddenly its owners had no time to take the signs down. As letters fall from old adverts and warning signs, they make a poetry for those who can recognise transformation: DANGER into ANGER. Anyone who comes to enjoy the sublime scariness of modern ruins (and you don't need to go to university to learn this stuff, any halfway decent horror film will teach you) can take back in pleasure some part of the surplus value used to build these places.

As well as ruins I have gone in search of micro-worlds, green routes in the city, signs of power and apocalypse, things around the fringes of heritage sites, phrases picked arbitrarily from books, the tops and subterranean parts of buildings, wormholes, North, 100-year-old oak trees, vertigo and childhood holiday memories. A walk might be helped or provoked by a theme, a quest, a burden, less often a destination. But I try to always be ready to change tack if the terrain offers a new and better theme.

Some very serious people will think that my walking is escapist (sometimes I wonder if they might be right), but most of the time it feels complex to me. It feels like a fight inside the fabrics of society for access to all those things that overdeveloped economies circulate at speeds just beyond our grasp: inner life, the wild absurdities of our unique and subjective feelings, beautiful common treasures, uncostable pleasures, conviviality, an ethics of strangerhood and nomadic thinking. Walking is pedestrian. Its pace disrupts things and makes them strange; like playing vinyl at the wrong speed. What otherwise flashes by, becomes readable, touchable, loveable, available. However, The Spectacle is not stupid; it has long been ready for such old-fashioned radicalisms, laying down huge and sugary sloughs of wholesomeness and holiness for us to founder in.... The Spectacle? Yes, the enemy of the sensitised walker (and of much more than that). And what is it? How does it smell? What does it look like? At what address can we find its headquarters?

The Spectacle is the growing Nothing in the lifeblood of society. It does not have a headquarters. With the advent of mass media in the twentieth century it manifested itself first as the dominance of images over things ("sell the sizzle not the sausage" as they said in 1950s TV advertising); since the coming of digital technology that virtualisation of life has increased and spread exponentially; what globalisation globalises is the Spectacle, the dominance of representations over what they represent. The Credit Crunch was caused by a crisis of intoxicated numbers not an overproduction of things. This is not to say that *things* are no longer produced; of course they are. But rather that it is the production of numbers and images that predominates. The vacuum left by things' fall from power sucks in our invisible private worlds and makes profits from them. We, the users, are the unpaid producers of vacuum-conglomerates like Facebook and Twitter: by our own labour we turn our love, opinions, intimacies, humour, lusts and family snaps into commodities. In 1990 I saw the new poor of post-Communist Eastern Europe literally selling their own underwear by the roadside; now we wash ours online. We have not all become groomed and digitised online-porn-addicted robots; we are resilient, but we are in a fight for the survival of the innerness of our inner lives, for the individuality of our individuality. The technology is not the problem. The problem is what organises most of it: a massive web of memes, ideas propagated for the sake of their own propagation, a programme for the accumulation of itself. This programme is the Spectacle: the dominance of the *ideas* of freedom, democracy, happiness over people actually being free, happy and democratically active; enforced by global deregulation of finance, the giant algorithms of the surveillance states, a media that has gone beyond mass to be more pervasive than gods were ever imagined to be, anti-collectivity laws and the war machines with their enemy-pals in the AK47 theocracies. Embodied and hyper-sensitised walking – with senses reaching inwards and outwards – is the antithesis of the Spectacle. The feeling body, alive with thoughts, is a resistance; theatre and insurgency combined. And what better and more unlikely cover than 'pedestrian'?

So, as I set out on each walk, it is always as if beginning a new round in a serious game, a spectral jousting with social fabrics that arm themselves with deceptive nonconformity, the smooth spiritual innerness of lounge music, and all the invented heritage, ancestry and bogus liveries of a mediaeval knight. Disturbingly, those fabrics often deploy the same tactics as me. That's why it's tricky...

I am very aware that I set off into all this from a grossly privileged position; with my partner I have to earn a living for our family, but I am not walking most of each day to fetch water. So I rely on you to translate whatever is of any worth here to your needs and circumstances, judging them through the prism of mine.

The 'great walk' I write about here, references the Great Work of the alchemists: a comparison borrowed from director Clive Austin's feature length movie *The Great Walk* in which he proposes that a more intense version of the kind of walking I am describing in this book is equivalent to the philosophical and spiritual search of the alchemists.

In my walking I seek to disrupt myself from my everyday life into all sorts of different dimensions, but then I always disrupt my disruptions and return abruptly to the everyday; I think this protects disruption from self-righteousness and helps to retain its powers to interrupt which would evaporate if interruption became a consistent principle.

Everyone will walk in their own different ways: some extrovertly and eccentrically, others in variations on what they think is a right way to walk. But to partake of a 'great walk', pleasure – free from obligations or commercial exchanges – is the first binding and common component, the criterion and the medium of the walk; guided less by maps and more by the intuiting of atmospheres and ambiences. It is by that intensely enjoyable (to the point of painfulness, sometimes) sensitisation to the emotional charge and change of space that I make my way.

My walking has long drawn on what I call mythogeography, with its key principles of multiplicity and trajectory. Applied to walking that means resisting routines and boundaries and treasuring the many selves you may pass through or encounter on your journey. I would always try to protect the freedom of walkers to use guises and camouflage in acts of transformation. In this cause, I sometimes find it necessary to adapt or détourn ideas and rituals taken from sacred spaces. There is always a place for an abstract or inner walk. But not to the exclusion of material interventions; hence, as I write, I am participating in the 'ambulant architectures' initiative of walking artists Wrights & Sites which seeks to equip walkers not only with concepts and tactics, but also with plain damned *things* for subtle and extravagant transformations of actually existing postmodernity.

There are a lot of ideas and images here. To keep them available as I explore, I set them in motion around me as if they and I were parts in an orrery (a moving model of the planets of the solar system) but without any sun at its centre, so each idea and tactic (and me) must find its own orbit and gather its own moons, making itself periodically available to be drawn upon where the circumstances of the road so encourage.

Each time I set out on one of my walks, I leave my home, disrupting myself from everyday life. (If I carry a phone it is never turned on; only there so my partner knows I can ring if I end up in a ditch with two broken legs.) No one knows where I am going; often least of all me. Walking out of our front door, I can go one of two ways. Either walk a narrow, stony footpath behind a terrace of houses down to a busy road, passing the ruins of a pub, in the foundations of which I can make out the flaky forms of a seam of Crackington Formation and enjoy the thought that I am beginning my walk passing over what was the floor of an ocean full of the very first sharks, some with ironing boards on their backs. Or, if I go the other way, I pass through an arch of purple volcanic rock, buried inside which, reputedly, is the body of an esoteric magician. Each of these beginnings throws a cast over my walks and I pass through their portals into an everyday already made strange and more than usually ready to be destabilised.

The walk I am about to take with you begins with a double dose of departure; because I first pay my respects to the magician and then turn the other way to slip down the path and walk across the sharks… and we are off…

*"Two or three hours walking will carry me to as strange a country
as I expect to see. A single farmhouse which I had not seen before is
sometimes as good as the dominions of the King of Dahomey."*
Henry David Thoreau

…just before we do set off together, maybe you would like to take a rest from words and walk for a while. So put down this book and walk. Or if you need something to get you started, or keep you going…

Walk upset
Walk spoiled
Walk spilled
Walk becoming ghost

Walk winningly
Parade up your own aisle

Carry your heart for a while
Cradle a deeper organ

Turn the map inside out and chew on it
Turn yourself inside out and get into things

Walk out
Walk as blank as you can
Again

Walk hand in glove with the thing you fear most
Calm palm plain smooth
Walk with rules
Walk to Ultima Thule
Waltz with two whatevers, a prospect, three narrows, a fraction and five notes
Walk wavy against rules
Walk towards sleep
Join the dots
Walk with 'yes'
Walk away

Murder a habit
Step off the other foot
Drop all you are
Fall
Leave
Trip yourself
Let go all you can
Step up

Lead a monster by the mind
Place each foot as if it were chosen
Walk with a companion you stitched together from body parts
Walk as if you are held together by your companion

Walk as if the road were rapids
As if your
As if
As

Praystep

Walk like water behind a dam
Walk released
Call into the grocery store as if it were your favourite museum
Walk like a breaker
Walk like a ball
Walk absurd
Walk unheard

Adopt a road as one of your major arteries
Swallow alley
Touch everything
Insert yourself into the wheel arches of wrecks, cold fireplaces,
empty coal bunkers, cubicles, secretly into beauty treatment
rooms, ditches, the margins of bowling greens and the gaps
between buildings

Walk as if Newton were right
Then as if Einstein is
Walk like a god particle
Walk like a stand-up
Walk like an erogenous zone
Walk like a canal
Walk as if everything were free
Walk in uncertainty
Walk in, as, like a field

Walk

My Sebald walk: Taken from my notebooks

No sooner had I begun to express an interest in the pleasurable potential of walking, than I was repeatedly advised to read novelist W. G. Sebald's **The Rings of Saturn.** *I resisted for some years (I do not find it easy to be told what to do) and when I did eventually get round to buying and reading the book I was not wholly seized by its account of a, supposed, walk through East Anglia until I came to Sebald's description of the former Atomic Weapons Research Establishment at Orford Ness and its surrounding terrain. I scribbled notes on every page, longing to visit these places. In Sebald's description, always tinged by the writer's melancholia, beneath the pall of the dog days of Saturn, I thought I recognised an extended landscape of dread: that quality of unsourced but containable panic that I had long identified as the preparatory excitement before a walk takes off into something like freedom.*

In 2011 I was in the middle of research that would result in my 'counter-tourism' initiative and looking for an opportunity to try out various visitor tactics on a range of heritage sites. I remembered Sebald's account of Orford Ness and found out that, since his walk there, it had been acquired by the National Trust. Coincidentally, I discovered around the same time that the town where my paternal grandfather had grown up and from where he had run away to join the army, is very close by. I resolved to replicate Sebald's walk, visit all the heritage sites along the way and maybe track down some remnant of a man who had said very little and whose voice I could no longer hear in my head. There might already be the start of a narrative: of walking through panic and melancholia to find a freeing of something. I mapped a 17-day walking route and booked into B&Bs for early summer. The week before I was due to set off I heard, on my phone, sitting on the bed in a London hotel room, on the eve of performing a walk in the Aldwych, that my mother's chemotherapy had not only been ineffective, but that her cancer was dramatically more advanced than anyone had suspected. I did the performance the next day and then went to be with my mother for the final three sad and joyous weeks of her lovely life.

After Mum's funeral, I came back home and re-booked the B&Bs for the autumn.

Posting my intentions to follow Sebald's path on Mytho Geography's Facebook page I received the following scarifying comments from two esteemed FB 'friends':

"I wrote as much as I need to on Sebald in my novel "69 Things To Do With A Dead Princess" - he's a bourgeois bigot: 'Alan castigated Sebald for telling the reader very little about Suffolk, and what he did have to say never rising above the level of clichés and inanities.'"

Stewart Home

"Lugubriously arriving at melancholy points you see coming a mile
off, with interchangeable winsome reflections."   Matthew Collings

*I perversely welcomed these adverse comments; though they stung at my purpose.
So many of the commentators I had read, without comprehension, were reverential
towards Sebald's work. I had come to feel that I was misusing a sacred tome as pretext
for a walk; now the book seemed more abject, ruined, something for me to salvage as I
read it along my way.*

I was deluded in every respect.

*For most of his working life a lecturer at the University of East Anglia, the
Bavarian-born W. G. ('Max') Sebald had famously rebuffed academic conventions
to explore the hinterland between the equally unstable provinces of fact and fiction.
Elusive of voice, methodically oblique, not writing about memory, but writing as if
memory itself remembered, a phantom biographer of the history that laughs behind
our backs when we think we have learned something from it, in prose woven and
unravelling but not necessarily in that order, elegant and anachronistic, unsure on the
boundaries where playfulness becomes deceit, Sebald seems to threaten knowledge of
the reader just as he seems most out of touch with himself.* **The Rings of Saturn** *was
an absurd map to take.*

And I deployed it absurdly.

*People had recommended Sebald's book in the same way as others had vouched
for Iain Sinclair's* **Lights Out For The Territory***; but only one was concerned with
geography. I knew nothing of Sebald's other work. I knew very little of his biography
and understood even less of his intellectual legacy. Until shortly before setting out,
for all I knew I might meet him on a quiet Suffolk lane. Without any sensible context, I
was following his text with no greater empathy and no less self-delusion than a stalker
following an obscure object of desire.*

On the eve of setting out I read Arthur Machen's **The Terror***, the narrative of
which briefly crosses my own intended route at Dunwich Heath. Machen's story is the
source for horror master H. P. Lovecraft's fictional 'Dunwich'. Lovecraft transposes the
town, a large East Anglian port mostly swept away by the sea in the early mediaeval
era, to Massachusetts for 'The Dunwich Horror', one of the core stories of his Cthulhu
mythos, with its god monster asleep in an inundated city. I had always regarded
Lovecraft's uncanny landscapes as some kind of mental map. It was only after my
walk that I discovered, in David Haden's* **Walking With Cthulhu: H. P. Lovecraft
as psychogeographer, New York City 1924-26***, that Lovecraft's night wanderings
in New York City, while deploying tactics not unlike my own (connecting ambiences,
camera mind, mania, carrying talismans), had informed the writer's invention of his
Cthulhu stories, with their back story of ancient, giant and, crucially, unspeakable
beings, obedient only to cosmic geometry, oscillating somewhere between geology
and organic mush, asleep and waiting in the sunken city.*

*I wrote down some quotations from Machen's story in my notebook, fragments
that were to assume a growing significance the deeper into East Anglia I walked.*

27.9.11

"I heard that a man living in Dunwich saw it one night like a black cloud with sparks of fire in it floating over the tops of the trees by Dunwich Common... "

"Land was to be bought... and secret excavations were to be made, till the country was literally undermined..."

"It was a dark mass against the sky, with wide spread boughs... in the depth of the dark of it points of fire... the dark tree lifted over the roof of the barn and rose up in the air and floated towards me..."

"the animals had revolted against men.... the horses were the murderers..."

"I believe that the subjects revolted because the king abdicated. Man has dominated the beasts throughout the ages, the spiritual has reigned over the rational... [But] for long ages he has been putting off this royal robe... He has declared... he is not spiritual, but rational, that is, the equal of beasts... the beasts... perceived that the throne was vacant... Hence, I think, the terror. They have risen once – they may rise again."

28.9.11

I leave the house for the railway station and enter The Mist. From this miasma emerges first the gothic bulk of the castle-like house at the top of our road and then the white modernist art deco elegance of the 'Mansions' flats to the side. Spectres in a spectre. No sooner out of the door than I enter inauthenticity: 'Taddyforde', the name of the big house, is an 1830s fabrication, replacing the plainer 'Taddiford' (the ford of toads) with something more olde worlde for a new gothic edifice.

Over the train's PA system the guard alludes to an "Indian Summer". The sun burns away The Mist as we cross the flat bottom of the valley and head towards London.

In order to enter the eternal present of W. G. Sebald's prose, I have left my Pop's (maternal grandfather's) watch, given in recognition of 25-years' service to Sterling Metals, on the bedside table. I have brought with me instead my Grandad's (paternal grandfather's) sniper's medal and the memory of his silence. My father has talked recently of how, despite listening to many tales of the army in India – of the annual march to the cooler north with the column headed by elephants, or of the weekly NCOs' dinner with its whisky carefully husbanded by the Sergeant Major – Grandad was always unwilling to speak a single word about the First World War. My father asked repeatedly and was always flatly rebuffed. For me Grandad *is* silence. I remember his hard white bristles, his huge hearing aid, and the dark heat of his council bungalow, but I cannot recall a single word spoken by him. He died when I was ten years old. I do not hear his voice. Will he speak to me if I find him in Suffolk?

I know, from Dad, that Grandad was a third or fourth son, born into a butchery and abattoir business in Halesworth, Suffolk, and that he somehow survived the four years of trench warfare. His ship, on its way back home from India, was diverted to France. Grandad had joined up to escape the prospect of always working under his elder brothers; an errand boy hauling parcelled meat. Was his sharpshooter's medal a clue to his survival: shooting men at long distance rather than charging 'over the top'?

There is an indifference to family history on Dad's side, the number of brothers is unclear, maiden names are forgotten, "lost touch" is a common phrase, no talk of rifts or conflicts but a dissipation of Smiths. All very different to the grand family gatherings and storytellings of my mother's side, the Oakleys. A cousin on my father's side, who is coming to the interment of Mum's ashes later this year, is worried about his own disconnection. His father died in a road accident, as did W. G. Sebald, as did Charles Hurst (the subject of my only other comparable walk), as did the Peace Pilgrim. In the movies a car crash is often followed by a silence.

"All tickets and passes, please." The guard moves through the train like a shiver.

The First World War is lost to us; death working its way through the veterans until only 'The Last Tommy' remained; bearing the whole symbolic weight. One day it will fall to someone, perhaps someone close to me, to be The Last Holocaust Survivor. And who will be The Last Bolshevik or have they gone already? The last passenger of the Windrush? The last 9/11 witness? Vast planes of silence condensing down to a single face. Pop. Gone. The train passes a large metal industrial unit with lettering in a deadpan font: **SOMERSET Heritage Centre**.

I have seen an intimate death this year, an unchosen but accepted, peaceful-inside-its-restlessness death. Silence after the last jerk, the hollow mouth. The loved gone. But industrial death, the abattoir, the trenches; them I can only approach through fakery and fiction, *The Terror*, Machen's burning tree-cloud, like fallout, that can lift itself up and over a barn, a plague of suffocating moths, a turning of the animals against the monarch-human, a return of the Irrational provoked by the abdication of the Material.

Outside the train the landscape is a terrible poised green, resentful of the train, tensing to spring, seething with Japanese Knotweed and Himalayan Balsam, towering over the track, a few fronds are snapped by the forward motion of the locomotive, but soon they get a hold, the green tentacles, like lophophores branching into more lophophores, seizing up the wheels, the engine trips and rolls end to end, the carriages jerked and then cartwheeling in the green arms of terror.

I am day-dreaming through this unnatural sward, deep and bright, in untimely late September sun, deep in economic crisis with the internet alive to a trader, fake or real it barely matters now, who says: "Goldman Sachs rules the world".

I begin to re-read *The Rings of Saturn*, surprised immediately that it is *after* Sebald's walk that he is taken into hospital in Norwich "in a state of almost total immobility". I had somehow re-imagined his walk as a convalescence, not a slow totter into complete collapse. This is a place I have already been to, carried from a classroom, immobile, supine, silent, 'unable' to speak, fake or real it barely matters now, the pretence becoming real as I lay for weeks on Nan and Pop's sofa, driven to hospital to have electrodes inserted in my scalp and lights flashed in my eyes. Then someone remembered that I had been hit on the head with a cricket bat; an explanation that absolved everyone. I didn't have to be mad, they didn't have to do anything.

A few years ago an Arts Council official described to me some theatre work I had done and then said: "ah, no, but that's the *other* Phil Smith!" I was gratified. Outside, the final fields before London flash by, like a film running backwards. I had misread Sebald, catastrophically. Thinking that he had walked *after* his immobility, as recuperation, and that I could repeat him, long after anything was at stake. Instead I will be walking *towards* immobility, towards the mush of real and fake again and again, already painfully aware that what I am doing is a copy of a copy of a copy. I am coming very late to join a long queue of repeated re-walkings and re-tellings of Sebald's 'original' journey, joining the back of the line behind the talking heads of Grant Gee's film *Patience (After Sebald)*, Iain Sinclair, Tacita Dean and all. They loom as if they have wandered, white-garbed, off the Olympian set of *Jason and the Argonauts*, but to ambient sounds rather than Bernard Herrmann. These demiurges, reflections in my train window, ease their opinions through static monochrome scenes that seem to have been peeled from the National Trust's calendar of haunted properties. I feel ignorant and uncomprehending against Katie Mitchell's mantra about perfect Sebaldian prose. A robotic somnambulist, I am following Sinclair's instruction to "just walk it"; knowing that to do so is to serve an immaculate sentence upon the sands and banal beauties of nuclear pagodas and bunkers that will kill us all.

The 'eternal present' of repetitions is one of many leaves sliding between each other in patchworks of fabrication: the questionable veracity of Sebald's story and the unwinding of my family history to name but two.

For a moment, I want to go back.

What I am gambling on seems very thin now: the simulacra of tourism, the halls of heritage mirrors, the idea that I might keep alive some spark by shifting these glasses to and fro, raising a sparkling tree over an old barn. What if I get stuck? Sunk in all that sand that I will always be walking on; the whole region is a prehistoric beach. Stuck in my own stupidity. What if I have backed the wrong horse? The murderer-horse? By copying too closely my Charles Hurst walk (in 2007 I had walked 200 miles following the route, a century before me, of an acorn-planting engineer, as I looked for his hundred-year-old oaks) have I gone a frame too far and pulled down the whole hall of mirrors and now am looking at the prospect of nothingness? Ivan texts. How do I make this thing work? What buttons do I push to make it readable? Can I turn this sparkling tree of panic into an efficacy? What kind of walking companions will Sebald's and Machen's horrors make? One's immaculate prose, the other's fallen spiritual aristocracy?

A brick pill box flashes by. What use is modulating chaos into a fiction of order, when what I really want to find is an enemy to the order of fiction: the dread that lifts the tree, the sea that inundates, the refusal that turns the animals fierce and strange? Another brick pill box; as my eyes are scanning Sebald's description of Thomas Browne's melancholic skull.

I have left my keys behind, with Pop's watch; I own nothing where I am going.

Sebald describes the spectators in Rembrandt's *The Anatomy Lesson* as gawpers, consumers of a spectacle, witnesses to a harrowing materiality that will impose itself on, and as, everything.

Two giant rectangles of flattened earth, cut out of the green of a field, served by a single link track from the distant road; forthcoming industrial units for storing surplus **'Heritage'** perhaps?

Sebald thinks it "odd" that the gawpers look not on the body, but at the medical book; surely as below so above, as then so completely now. Sebald's 'eternal present' is the history of the Spectacle, the synchronic imaging of bodies, the reduction of mess, swarm, sward and invasion to a pixilation. The dead man's mouth, the empty openness, serving no express purpose, silenced...

Walking bodies

TRYING TO EVEN THINK, let alone write about, what my body does during a walk is like trying to study an octopus while engaging in a fight with it.

J. Scott Turner suggests in his book *The Extended Organism: The Physiology of Animal-Built Structures* that we should consider the farthest edges of our bodies to include those structures, however insubstantial or artificial, that affect the flow of energy to and from the body, in fact anything that "adaptively modifies flows of matter through the environment" and more particularly between the extended organism and the environment. He suggests that we reject the conventional model of an organism's border as "a thing" and better regard it as "a process.... conferring upon the organism a persistence that endures as long as its boundary can adaptively modify the flows of energy and matter through it". This suggests that we should be far more wary of drawing a line between our body and everything else.

The modern mind is porous to the influence of attractively advocated memes, to exterior ideas of a 'self' lurking behind our eyes, and is physically evolved for synthesising and juxtaposing its understanding of objects, animals and humans; so perhaps the whole body, extended, is similarly open and synthesising. Mythogeography, my ambulatory philosophy, regards the body as being as much a site as its geological and architectural surroundings and equally 'conscious'. A site we perform upon, on and in, is ambiguously a costume, a shop, a stage, a terminus.

A functionless walk is about as embodied as you can get. Easing, waiting, responding, jerking, rolling, smoothing, tip-toeing the body across the environment. It would be a shame if, after all the erotic energy expended by people 'getting in touch with nature', no one really touched it. So handle the weft and weave, the detail, the spiny thorn and the nettle hair. Leave a little of your blood on things. Take stones home in bruises. Test clay between your fingertips. Put your head in rivers. Let tadpoles and tiny crabs scuttle across the back of your arm.

Stand still to feel the different kinds of wind; let them push you, walk against them.

Tread (with the right boots) on bottle fragments and tin cans. And then spend a few minutes enjoying the textures after the crunch. You don't always have to be precious.

There may be a tendency to place your focus, your 'centre', in the brain wobbling on the stalk of your spine; so experiment with shifting that focus into your ankles or wrists or knees or hips; become a thing of joints and hinges and allow your thoughts and feelings to model them. Thinking with your feet is not about 'groundedness', but rather about rediscovering legs as feelers, tentacles, bio-instruments that complement the meshwork of senses that bathe and caress the surfaces about us with exploratory seeing and touching and smelling and hearing and tasting, all the time swinging the whole body of instruments through the hips. Conduct your senses like an orchestra, reconnecting the two parts of your body in a swaying walk, use your stride to disperse longings to the landscape.

Allow the focus of your self-consciousness to unravel like an unfurling proboscis, to ripple like lophophores on lophophores, to explore and propel like tentacles.

When I read what Rebecca Solnit writes in her book *Wanderlust, A History Of Walking* about a rooted "return" to the body's "original limits", of the return of a "supple" and "sensitive" body against postmodernism's passive, medical/erotic body, decentralised and fragmented…

I feel uneasy.

When she writes "on foot everything stays connected, for while walking one occupies the spaces between…. interiors in the same way one occupies those interiors: one lives in the whole world rather than in interiors built up against it…"

I feel uneasy.

An overriding quality of walking, particularly in the city, can be its connectedness. But not at the expense of disruption, of tripping up and over, stumbling and righting, of falling, of refusal, of risking the crossing, of not looking, of disrupting the flow, of not going to the destination… that it is also in these disconnections that the enigmatic meanings of the city and the landscape can be floated free from their immobile sites and engaged in a movement that may eventually lead them back to connections, but not to begin with, not quite yet. Don't rush it.

…"that's it," I said as Mum died, before closing her eyes and kissing her goodbye.

Recently I was in the old anatomy theatre at King's College London, off the Strand, where we dissected a guided tour of the City led by Mel and James from ecological artist-activists 'Platform', uneasy at its prioritising of the transfer of information over the affects and immersions of our embodied journey. I am embarrassed to remember my comments, beginning only now to own up to myself about the formalism of my Aldwych tour, its marginal, cowardly and evasive siting. The participants recall it warmly, as if it was wholly contentless.

This morning our house was surrounded in the Great Fog of 1674, the white Mist that rises from a "body opened presently after death" and that clouds the brain when sleeping. And is dispelled now by the bright blinding light of an Indian Summer. Did I dream the voice on the radio as I woke: "though God forgives, the markets do not"?

Sleep and The Mist and the cowardly turns of my walks are my sparkling terrors, burning me back from the road's dynamic patterns; their bright irrationality, haziness and romanticism only so much quibbling over terms. So, even my misgivings are held in bad faith. Then are the monsters, mutations and deformities I hold so dear no more than a wrangling over the terms of what is already lost; that even these mistakes are parts of a pattern in which every revelation leads "without fail down into the dark"? Surely, there is some efficacy in what Thomas Browne so strenuously decries: "an ever-widening, more and more wonderful arc"?

I have come through the underground, through Liverpool Street Station; the train to Norwich will be pulled by an engine named 'Royal Anglian Regiment'. It just blooped into life. I climb on and find a seat at a table. The train from Exeter was named after a train driver. Just now, outside Liverpool Street Station, searching for a quiet place to return Ivan's call, I found myself in "Hope Place", a memorial site to the Kindertransport, the child refugees who passed through this station, a key historical reference point in W. G. Sebald's final novel: *Austerlitz*. The 'Gherkin' looms. I am reminded that Liverpool Street Station was designed by J. D. Dewsbury's father, and I recall the moment that J. D. (geographer and non-representational theorist) and I walked through the station to the beginning of that guided walk around the City with 'Platform'. He spoke of hardly knowing his father, who died when he was young (I think of Grandad) and of the strangeness of passing through the place, knowing how his father's plans here were compromised. That day, J. D. was nursing a stitched mouth, treating it with painkillers. Today I catch myself standing in the concourse of the station, un-focusing my eyes, and seeing the people as patterns, shaped by the exits and entrances, by the flows encouraged and inhibited, standing for a while in the compromised patterns of the mind of J. D.'s father...

Tactics of sensitivity

DURING A WALK, I can draw on numerous tactics; notions and tasks that I have picked up or devised over the years and now keep in my head as resources. The device I used in Liverpool Street Station helped to sensitise me to certain flows and patterns. Key to my walking has been this sensitising. Not a spectacular sensual overload, but mostly subtle devices, games and refrains for peeling away a layer of armour, extending a sympathetic organ or opening the eyes a little deeper. Here, before I rejoin my walk following Sebald, are some more of my sensitising tactics and notions:

⊤ Senses

Carry, touch, inhale, sip, rub and lick things as you find them... over two years Lawrence Edmonds licked parts of all 64 Anglican cathedrals in the UK.

⊤ Repetition

Walk the same short route again and again.

After the initial excitement, then passing through a phase of seeing only the same things, new things should begin to emerge around the time you decide there is nothing more to be seen.

Walking one street repeatedly and together, it was only after many weeks that Simon and I noticed that the 'weed' in the gap between the pavement and café wall was a tomato plant and that it was growing a single tiny bright red fruit. Abdullah, one of the owners, said he thought it might have come from the seed of a fried tomato dropped by a customer.

⊤ Walking in situ

Alone, walk the street or the hill path or the beach into yourself. This is not an opportunity to empty psychic garbage onto the world.

This is a psycho-geographical act, raising and reforming memories, feelings, self-images and setting them at the mercies of the far vistas, of the straightness of the path, of the massing of the flocks above.

Allow all those inner things nattering in your heart and head to be softly contoured by the dale, torn apart by corvine parliaments, strictly bordered by barbed wire fences, faced down by mountains and high rises.

⊤ Eye, eye

Do you meet the world head on? When you see a stranger on the path up ahead do you look them in the eye, beyond them, to the side, at their feet, at their breasts, their ass, their pockets, their hands, their labels, their lunchpack or their sixpack?

Are you challenging, inviting, deadpan, oppressive, invasive? Do you look at the shopfronts or the storeys above them? Do you look up to the hill tops as if there were gods vacationing there or do you meet them straight in the eye; as trusted friends or respected enemies? Or do you look down on everything and everyone?

⊤ Step up

Find a pavement slab, an empty plinth, or a doorstep for which there is no longer a house, and once a day, a week or a year get down on your hands and knees and wash or polish it (unless this is something you are usually obliged or paid to do, in which case spend the time doing something you want, and others don't want you, to do).

"Our hands are also our feet." (Tadashi Suzuki)

⊤ Somatic specific

Take care to place your attention thoughtfully. Let your focus run out to the horizon and then back to the ground between your feet. Look closely at the texture of a wall or a tree, while holding up a hand to feel the snow, the wind, the heat of the sun.

Hold things close as you look at something in the middle distance. Stretch your focus, dissolve false boundaries on your attention. Imagine yourself as a listening device. Or a steadicam. Allow metaphors to direct your senses: you see a forest, let your limbs be guided by the winds for a while. You see a tap: feel out in waves of looking. Bend and leap to touch things not within your immediate reach. Use your whole body as you explore; be directed by a tingling in your skin, follow a scent.

Do not limit your responses to your experiences to literal ones; your feelings are as ambiguous and allusive a set of materials as imagist poetry, so interpret them appropriately. Mix up your senses; look for red sounds or quiet aromas. Keep varying the height of your head from the ground. Lie down in a city street and take the perspective of a rough sleeper for a moment. Carry a light plinth for looking over walls. In shopping areas check out the storeys above the generic ground floor shop fronts.

Every now and then stand stock still and listen carefully, identifying as many different sounds as you can. Interweave physical variations – low and high, far and near – with the narrative of a walk; as shadows lengthen direct your focus further and further from you; visit a row of flower shops and then search out the scents of the shops that do not sell flowers.

⊤ Fear

Fear is OK. Ill at ease is OK. Getting badly hurt is not. Being too scared to do what you should do is not. Most threats are not real. I am afraid of dogs; all dogs. It probably has something to do with my almost becoming dogmeat for a cat-eater called Prince (my Pop's hound); I think he saw my pram as an opened tin of Kennomeat. It is not pleasant to feel fear as I hear a bark or the sound of claws scratching on a path, but there is a release later. A rhythm of tension and relaxation, a hyper-sensitised mapping of a (mostly very thin) threat layer along with other, more enjoyable, layers of poignancy and discovery. Embrace these containable and mostly irrational fears as part of the uncomfortable music of your walk.

⊤ Walking as other

Walk as a detective; you don't know what the crime is, but you know that everyone is a suspect. You are the first zombie of the apocalypse; you are the final human survivor. You are fox, ghost, spy. Walk as Cupid, pairing in your head one stranger with another. You went to heaven or hell (you guess) and this is it. A miner tunnelling through overground seams, a minor character in a thriller trying to slip out of view; you are walking underwater... don't act these out, but hold the feeling and the fiction in your head as you walk through the scenarios.

⊤ Landscapes beyond desire

Walk the landscape as if it were a body – sensitise yourself to its warming, stiffening, puckering, relaxing, folding, arching, ejaculating, excreting, shuddering, shivering, flooding.

⊤ Touch things

Just touch things.

⊤ Our enemies...

...are not each other. But the homogenisation, policing and reduction of multiplicity.

⊤ In the city

The hubs and nodes of large cities are often crowded. By consciously sensitising yourself to others in these busy spaces you can turn your walks through the crowds into a dance or a sport; making complex steps, incorporating everyone else into your choreography, intuiting and pre-empting patterns of trajectories and velocities, picking the gap just as it opens, and just before it closes.

With practice you will cultivate an eye for a developing crisis, signs of flocking and cues for approaching issues; you will soon find a capacity not simply to avoid problems, but to catch a person as they faint, to meet a gaze from a hundred metres away, to direct a lost language student without breaking stride, to pretend to hide behind lamp posts when you see your very best friends far off, to play.

Once you have begun to sense the patterns you can start to move beyond being simply responsive, and to work as a dramaturg of the streets; provoking crises, waltzes, spontaneous symposia, and elegant and massive eddies in crowds.

(A word of caution: sensitising yourself to the flows of the city will not redeem you from or inure you to its violent commerce. The very opposite: experience and subjectivity are exactly what are most fiercely traded now. Rather than releasing you from the clutches of overdevelopment, sensitising tactics are intended to bring you right into the belly of the Spectacle.)

...earlier, at Paddington, the myths had begun to draw themselves up and there was a moment of supernatural agency. Passing through the gates towards the underground platform I realised I was no longer carrying my copy of *The Rings of Saturn*. In a panic, slapping my jacket pockets, the book, as if from thin air, leapt from around the area of my elbow and I caught it before it hit the platform. I had no memory of transferring it there. It was as though for the time I had forgotten it, it had both sustained and suspended its presence, quite independent of any agency of mine, only reappearing at the return of my memory of it. As though it intended to resist my attempts to tame it by dissection and critique, and would fight for its integrity as a vibrant thing; demanding my constant attention. On the train out of London, two lads are watching a movie on a laptop. Two Mormon black suits get on at Chelmsford. The badge of one says his name is Elder Wolf. One of my knees begins to ache...

Knees

PLENTY GETS WRITTEN about feet and walking. Little about knees. Perhaps we are all hoping that if we ignore them they will behave themselves.

I would almost certainly not be writing about knees now, but for carrying a knee injury during the time I was assembling these texts. I was forced to notice, by limping, how changing the axis through which the knee swings the body alters the walker's relation to the ground and everything else around. Rather than an apparently smooth passage of optic flow and thought, everything is broken up by stride-sized punctuations; the centre of the body sinks too and swings around and to the beat of pain.

All the habits of hyper-sensitisation described above have had to be re-learned; I had to teach myself to think in short phrases, then joining them together, pushing the centre of my feeling out into the world again. Rather than tiredness or stiffness of muscles that can be eased or rested, or blisters on soles or heels that can be alleviated by blister-plasters or allowed to heal or just walked through, an injury to a joint can feel like a prelude to stopping completely, as if a key principle has broken down or been found to be false, that one has been caught out, the first halt in a catastrophic seizing up, the coming to rest of all one's walking.

A creaking, speaking memento-mori carried inside the walker, sending out cranky, malfunctioning signals and re-angling trajectories.

There is a kind of high risk jouissance here, on the edge of everything suddenly seizing up and ending. An unpredictability around which my future hinges. Rather than taking for granted that I can at any time pull on my boots and set off for twenty miles of wandering, now I am grateful for each and every step and choose them and treasure them more carefully than ever before.

...Nic Green at the launch of 'Making Routes' in Glasgow last week spoke of walking on very little food, falling asleep in the afternoon beside a river and waking to find that she had been joined by an otter. A girl listening to an iPod jigs on the platform at Colchester. She wears a Beatles tee-shirt. Eternal present.

I feel the land change after Manningtree; rusted containers in the sward guarded by lightning trees, huge expanses of derelict factory and skeletal bird hides. More dread, less clear, The Mist is invisible here. What intangible masks am I bringing? What if the circulation of ideas around a walker's head, their hyper-attention to detail and narrative (without falling into clinical paranoia)...

Crab Man's razor

A COMMON RESEARCH PROTOCOL is Occam's Razor: the idea that the simplest explanation is the likeliest. Turn this around and adopt, no matter how fragmentary and partial your evidence, the most complex, sinister and portentous explanations possible until disproved by further evidence. Check out the secret codes on manhole covers. You might also adopt a complementary Fortean approach: assuming that the greatest significance is to be found among anomalies and minorities.

...making connections between things that cannot (apparently) be rationally connected, with those things already in motion. What if all that which has been such a force of illumination on previous walks should suddenly wrap itself up into a mist of bandages around my head? Hit on the head with a geography; no connections, absolving everybody. Reading Sebald writing of *Urn Burial*, a book by Thomas Browne, I wonder if Liverpool Street Station might be a giant urn to and partly by J.D.'s father? Is it the nature of all architecture to be our funerary ornaments? I learned from my mother's dying, from her *way* of dying, her chosen attitude to what she could not choose, that your dying is a legacy to those who remain, a memorial of, in Mum's case, unfrightened contentment, completion, gratefulness and ordinary gracefulness. So, if our living body is our urn, as much a construction as the buildings it lives in, then we walk in our own memorial and what we make and do as we live are just as much memento mori for others as how we die. In the fields an obscene stump, neither natural nor manufactured; a phallus of tiles.

Once in Norwich, I ring Ivan and we approximate an arrangement to walk together on Saturday or Sunday. I soon find the church of St Peter Mancroft and it is full of sunlight. I locate the memorial to Thomas Browne. A small group of middle-aged singers are sat in a circle. One, as if speaking from a script, says: "Beauty is that quality when a group of people unite around a single object and become more than what they are apart." The tunes they sing are irritatingly simple. From a text in a display case I gather that a plaster-cast of Thomas Browne's skull, one of five taken, is in the sacristy of the church, along with the case used for the display of the original in the hospital museum. (As I write this I am biting into a puri that explodes its sweet contents across my mouth...)

Don't take your own food

UNLESS YOU ARE walking in a wilderness and do not know how to hunt or scavenge, do not take your own food. Allow the food to come to you. I do not plan my meals or take supplies for the road, but try to put myself at its mercy. I would rather walk hungry past reheated mediocrity – not on health, but entertainment, grounds – than spurn the chance to once more stumble upon baba ghanoush, gâche, peas and mint sauce, homemade faggots, salt beef or some other unplanned delicacy. Just as that food will taste all the richer for discovery, so the same applies to the narrative of the journey.

Coming unexpectedly upon an abandoned fairground or the skeleton of an industrial unit will always have far more thrill than a planned and guided trip around a stately home. When the context is ordinary, a slight shift in ambience, the sight of some small thing in profound decay or the meeting of a lilo and a bacon slicer on a forecourt, can trigger deep, deep satisfaction.

...just like the beach food described to me by Anjali when she joined me for one of my *Crab Walks* in 2004. Her portrayal of the boy/woman Islamic chemist Djaq in the latest TV *Robin Hood* has made her even more a limited myth for me; ambiguous, multiply-layered and part of a drifting gang. I wash down the sweetness with salty lassi.)

At the west door of the church is a large, elderly, sleeping guide dressed in surgical boots. I make another circuit of the church in the hope that he will wake. When I return he is still slumped, so I decide to take his picture; turning on my camera, it makes a jingling sound, and he rouses. I say to him: "I hear a cast of the skull of Thomas Browne is in the sacristy. Is it closed or would I be able to view it?"

As I speak these words the expansive guide's eyes repeatedly turn up into their sockets. But he revives when I reach the question mark and, vigorously replying "NO! THAT would NOT be possible today!" his head slumps violently onto his chest and, before I can thank him, he plunges back into unconsciousness, perhaps even abruptly, parodically, passing away.

I wander into the big glass Forum building. In the library I find the Memorial Collection of a US Air Force Bomber division; in display cases there are numerous models of bombers in bright abstract-expressionist liveries.

I think at first that they must be the product of an Artist's Residency, but, no. These patterns were used to help bomber formations of up to a thousand planes at a time identify each other and assemble in low light or in the dazzle of bright sun, the symmetry of their formations being crucial to "effective bombing": the setting of firestorms in civilian areas. These bright jazzy patterns are the livery of industrialised killing, remembered to Sebald by a gardener at Somerleyton Hall, a history occluded by the publications on these firestorms by Holocaust denier, antisemite and racist David Irving, absolving the rest of us from examining and accounting for them.

No connection.

From the quiet vantage point of the Indian vegetarian cafe, enjoying the Indian Summer's day, now on the 'wrong' side of the river, I watch a hugely-drunk man attempt the nimble-fingered task of rolling a cigarette. He ends up rolling off his seat and falling onto his hands and knees; his clowning reminds me of Sebald struggling from his hospital bed and crawling on all fours to take a look out of his window.

The drunk man, back on his bench, takes a very careful sip of Special Brew and places the can with a bomber's precision beside him on the seat. A young woman stops and rolls a cigarette for him. A small act of kindness.

On my way to St Peter Mancroft I had passed Hardwick House, a bank built in 1866; hardly was it open than it was sunk in scandal. One of the owners was caught running fake accounts against which he was borrowing to fund high-risk, high-return speculations (thank heavens such a crime could not be committed today; such practices having long formed the basis of legal speculation). It was the financial instability of the Franco-Prussian War of 1870-1 (read Iraq/Afghanistan, 2001-11) that exposed the fraud at Hardwick House...

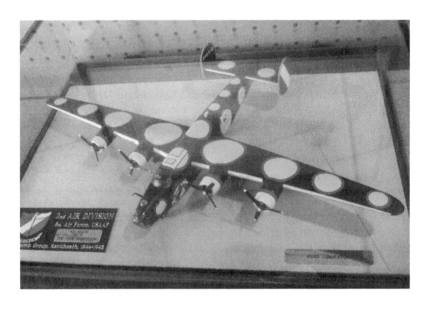

A skill...

...WORTH CULTIVATING is Fortean speed reading; a nose for very quickly sourcing and identifying the quirky pamphlet or special chapter of speculative and anomalous materials, then running a finger across its text to pick the cherries. Training yourself to have only five minutes in a bookshop or library to find the thing you need. To do that surveillance thing of having a list of trigger words in your head: "butcher", "nuclear", "sunken"... a different list for each walk. On a quest you have no time to be reading every word of long volumes; treat books and websites as bran tubs. As capitalists treat banks.

...the bank's creditors were bailed out, the building bought by the state for a post office. Everything about the building speaks of permanence, fabricated beyond the span of human lives, a cathedral of capital; yet it lasts a few years, a fragile urn.

How long will memories of Mum's death remain and how long before memories of her life return?

I work out that Hardwick House was the headquarters of Anglia Television at a time when the company produced its mockumentary *Alternative Three*; I will be listening for echoes of its paranoid tale of terrorised scientists and the militarisation of space.

I am due to meet Lorraine at the railway station tomorrow; what are the tactics for our visit to Somerleyton Hall to be? Should we try to blur the natural with the manufactured, to blur ourselves as natural with the manufactured, to be touristic objects ourselves, to be the things of heritage tourism, surreptitiously placing ourselves in display cases? To be hero and heroine; to undo an historic wrong? Of course, that is to make ourselves monsters.

I go to see the film *Drive* at Cinema City; the lovely, smiling hero whose currency is smooth but devastating violence; he is a true monster like Long John Silver or a bomber commander pulling the temple down.

Walking across Norwich I pass a tiny, isolated mediaeval house in the middle of a car park, sandwiched between tall modern offices. The B&B I'm staying in, The Gothic House (from gothic to gothic today), is equally an anomaly: in a multi-ethnic, working class area, a sliver of Strawberry Hill.

On the way back from the movie, I glimpse an ominous scene through an office window. A visceral and violent consultancy, a storming of brains, all around a rectangle, every hair in place, sales people, corporate strategists. I check the name on the door plate: 'The Writers' Centre, Norwich'.

The TV in my room at The Gothic House does not work.

39

A few highlights from other drifts and wanders (1)

ᵞH̩ Coming face to face with a tiger in the woods above Zurich.

ᵞH̩ On a very first drift, finding the water tower for the old asylum encased in thick brambles; a find that gave that wander both narrative and adventure.

ᵞH̩ In searing sunlight after a storm, Anoushka and Katie in the far doorway of a barn making a silhouette of two tea-drinking ladies; using their bodies and pieces of cardboard. "Do you think they're real?" a passing group of enchanted women walkers asked me in a whisper.

ᵞH̩ Simon saying "rural walking is boring" the moment before we saw through a gate a field full of the remnants of demolished houses (with which we played for the next two hours).

ᵞH̩ Giddy with the heat, leading a fear-frozen horse by its bridle, me scared too, at the request of its unnerved rider, across a road, glancing up to see the massive eye of alarm just above me.

ᵞH̩ An angry man who thought we were surveyors come to put a building on his community's last piece of green land (a grassed decoy pond); after we had reassured him he invited us all into his garden for cake and tea, and I saw in the stream at the bottom of his garden an eel battling upstream.

ᵞH̩ Talking about Horatio Nelson, when over my shoulder peered a one-eyed man.

ᵞH̩ With Karen, finding a peacock transfixed by its own image in a roadside mirror.

ᵞH̩ A tyre warehouse ablaze in the dark hours of the morning.

ᵞH̩ A huge pool of blood spilled across a suburban street in Fribourg.

⁷Ḥ Crossing an abandoned racecourse in the middle of a Belgian wood.

⁷Ḥ With Polly and Simon, finding a barn full of sheep listening to jazz.

29.9.11

"For the valley of the Waveney I see the vale of Tenoctitlan, for the slopes of Stowe the snowy shapes of the volcanoes Popo and Iztac, for the spire of Earsham and towers of Ditchingham, of Bungay, and of Beccles, the soaring pyramids of sacrifice gleaming with the sacred fires, and for the cattle in the meadows the horsemen of Cortes sweeping to war." This is from *Montezuma's Daughter* by H. Rider Haggard, who wrote at Ditchingham Hall, which is on my route. I have raided it from the shelves of my B&B bedroom, along with *I Walked By Night*, a poacher's autobiography ghosted by Rider Haggard's daughter, Lilas, and other volumes of 'local interest'.

I learn that the anchorite Julian of Norwich in her cell participated in the liturgy through a squint in the wall: can I find squints in Norwich through which to participate in the liturgy of the city? "Fear not the language of the world"; George Borrow grew up here, taught to wander by the gypsies he ran away with. "Under the West Norwich streets there are old chalk workings. They open up occasionally and a bus disappears…" (D.J. Taylor, *Real Life*).

Perhaps Lorraine and I should walk the Hall as if its floors are made of ice or glass?

In nearby Wright's Court eight bodies were piled, dead from diphtheria, the illness Mum survived, contracted simultaneously with TB; she passed on an immunity to me. When the gravediggers returned to the pile, the body of an elderly woman on the top had disappeared. Does it still walk? Hauntings at 19 Magdalen Street, close by, formerly a brothel, a girl strangled; a ghost disturbs bags of clothes in the charity shop, folding them neatly and stacking those suitable for a young woman.

My walk is framed by its postponement due to Mum's dying and by the interment of Mum's ashes a few days after the walk's intended completion.

Obelisks in the breakfast room; rays of light frozen in stone. The coffee jug is an urn. The holder of brown and tomato sauces a grave. The butter knife an Egyptian death tool; the mouth-opener. At breakfast, an episodic tale, disrupted by bacon; a grain of truth in every 'family legend'.

The bran flakes holder explodes in my hands and I surreptitiously clear up the mess between chapters of the owner's tale of all he knows about his house. An island of Regency in a pub yard, The Gothic House is a narrow, almost freestanding, three-storey, multi-story building. What its owner has to say about it is not remarkable, but his way of saying it is; his prose is as complex and interwoven as anything by Sebald, if not quite so worked. The owner presents solid evidence and then reveals it to be mistaken, then family hearsay which he mocks and subsequently resurrects, local rumour which he undoes before reclaiming it.

Through his tale he weaves three mayors who become one mayor in public service three times and a mistress hidden away with her maid who, together, become a respectable French governess and her daughter. Some of his deductive leaps leave him short of the far side, but his aim is never for a bridge of logic but rather a setting of many points in motion about each other simultaneously. He describes what he is doing as arranging a few pieces of the jigsaw. I say to him that the problem with the past is that there is never any flat surface on which to arrange the pieces. Half way through my fried egg I realise that I have found, already, one of those special characters who unexpectedly people these walks from time to time...

Encounters

Ascended

ON MY WALK in the footsteps of the acorn-planting Charles Hurst I met a woolly-hatted psychogeographer who drove a JCB. In half an hour of conversation, he took me on an imaginary journey through underwater ballrooms and plague villages and along roads to nowhere.

In Guernsey I met a man who levered himself along the cliff top on crutches. While photographing the sea, he described to me in detail how the island was run by a mafia. I turned down his offer of a lift because I wanted to see things on foot, but maybe that was a mistake.

In a Tibshelf graveyard I nodded to a woman who burst into tears. I looked into her empty eyes. I helped her to find a place to bury her dying husband: a miner whose role as a conduit for a divine source of inspired words she was preparing to assume.

Outside a pub in a Nottinghamshire village a woman pulled down her blouse to show me the purple bruising of heart massage, pointed to the pavement and, unknowingly repeating words from Hitchcock's *Vertigo*, said: "and there I died".

All the time we have the chance to meet extraordinary folk, but they do not necessarily immediately appear exceptional. So when a Dersu Uzala (as in Akira Kurosawa's movie of that name) comes to your campfire like a bear out of the darkness, try not to turn him or her away. At any one time there are only seven Ascended Mistresses or Masters at work on the Earth, so it would be a shame to turn one away, particularly as you cannot find them by looking; without anonymity they would not be what they are.

> *"of course there are always a few psychopaths, but mostly there are fallen angels"*

Suspended sentience

WALK AS IF THE CITY, the river, the sea, the field were sentient beings. Walk as if you were a city, a river, a sea, a field.

Demilitarisation

Jooyoung Lee, an artist who often uses walking in her work, has set up a Fantasy Real Estate office; a pseudo estate agents, as a means to visit a place that is unwalkable for most people; 'customers' pay a visit to the 'office' to inspect, through maps and documentation, the ruined sites of the demilitarised zone between North and South Korea.

Doppelgänger

What do you do when you meet yourself coming the other way?

"destiny is the enemy"

...we are on the train now, as it passes through the villages south of Norwich, ticking off the route's landmarks described in Sebald's book. Lorraine, once a colleague in my home city, a teacher of autobiographical theatre and a volunteer in my counter-tourism research, tells me how the journey to Machu Picchu of the American explorer Hiram Bingham III was tracked by the native Indians. Bingham had believed he was battling through an empty jungle; but his progress would be woven into their tapestries.

I wondered about fictions we might be parts of, yet never get to read; or if we did, would not recognise ourselves in them.

Lorraine tells me how her Mum gives tours of her house to friends who call for the first time; Lorraine's childhood tartan kilt, now a cushion, is the prop her mother uses to accompany a description of her first meeting with Lorraine's Scottish father, lost in Hampton Court maze. No photos or actual artefacts are used on these tours; the properties are abstract.

We complete the journey to Somerleyton Hall on foot along quiet roads, accompanied by bees, deer and heron. I miss the red squirrel that Lorraine sees. We stand silently under the tree up which it has fled; everything soundless but for the crinkle of dry leaves.

A potato truck passes.

On an obscure green, Lorraine circumambulates an incongruous memorial post, fifteen feet tall, marking the development of the hovercraft.

We are walking a terrain of cubby holes and hideaways; a woman we ask the way talks of "glebe land", military technology, rural idyll and longstanding property.

At Norwich Station I had pointed out to Lorraine the hospital building in the distance where Sebald had been admitted and Lorraine had pointed out that it had been demolished a few years previously. Crowds had gathered to see the blocks pulled down; folk took bits as keepsakes, nostalgic for a past many of them had never had. Joseph Campbell writes of the myth of the "overgrown" that actually hides nothing.

Entering the grounds of Somerleyton Hall, Lorraine and I flounder for a while. My suggested tactics have no purchase at all. We admire a tree blown over in the 1987 hurricane, levered back up again and still growing. We sit down within an enclosed bower in the gardens, half-amused at the lack of a view and here we talk of death and loss and the South American (Lorraine's mother is from Peru) practice of holding regular remembrances of the dead. The Reformation ended that here; after a funeral, ritual is silenced.

Anticipating the pleasure of a mischievous adventure, I am instead rediscovering my discomfort with conventional heritage sites.

Lorraine describes how her Indian father-in-law disrupted a visit to a National Trust property by his over-responsiveness; roaring with laughter on being told that the champagne glasses on display were modelled on Marie Antoinette's breasts, upbraided for collecting herbs from the kitchen garden. We plunge into the official tour, inserting our boots into blue overshoes to protect the carpets. Samuel Morton Peto, the first owner, "was ruined by the banks".

When Lorraine found me this morning at the station I was trying to meet the stare of a bust of Peto in the station at Norwich; his gaze so lofty it would have required a ladder to succeed.

The jingoism of the tour is crude: "I hope none of you are French, ha ha..."
...mais, bien sûr, motherfucker. Otherwise, the guides are amiable enough, enjoying themselves, and although there is no account of what is at work here, no hypotheses, no dynamic patterns, no organising ideas, yet there is such a plethora of disconnected details that disconnection itself serves as the misty logic that connects them all. The Order of the Cloud and Banner serves up tales of Wellington and Nelson (the latter's body kept in spirits later drunk by his sailors), and of a tunnel and a maze, of the crosses on the Crossley carpets (are we trampling the Cross?), and of compasses (was the first owner a freemason?) These are the beginnings of stories without middles or ends.

The guides reveal a painting of the present Lady of the house; its subject wrapped in a sheet to emphasise her décolletage. They describe how on seeing this image, the present Lord requested an introduction from the painter to his sitter. The story and the image do not quite fit, as if a clumsy conjurer had dropped his cards; they hover like the shadows of a mechanical process in a space between otherwise subtle things. Telling a charming story, the guides tell a story of charming.

The retired Lord Somerleyton, still resident somewhere in the grounds, arranged visits by heads of state: Mitterrand and Reagan we are told... but Ceauşescu too? Presumably? One of the powers behind quaint titles: the Master of the Queen's Horse, a Lord In Waiting. A safe pair of hands. There is a zodiac in the centre of the lawn; a magical mapping of colonial ambitions that stretch to the stars, marking and possessing the heralds and the myths that drive them, the archangels and their natures that influence the planetary bodies: Moon-Gabriel, Mars-Samuel, Mercury-Raphael, Jupiter-Zadriel, Venus-Angel, and Saturn-Cassiel, the angel of solitude and tears, a traveller with the power to make others wander aimlessly, one of the choir of angels called The Powers, he who presides over the death of kings...

Democracy

THERE IS AN OCCULT astronomical map that everyone has access to. At all times, passing through our bodies are microwaves that are part of what is called the Cosmic Microwave Background radiation. These are the ripples of energy left over from the Big Bang. Because the universe expanded from such a tiny, dense mass, these waves pass through everything, everywhere.

Scientists have been measuring them for decades in projects like BOOMERANG, COBE and the Planck Cosmology Probe; they have detected, in ways that can be plotted against the sky, tiny variations of temperature within the microwaves. When these miniscule anomalies are mapped, they reproduce the grand structures of the universe; a wrinkle in a microwave mimes a galaxy. Whoever we are, passing through our bodies at all times, is a map of the entire universe.

...and Sun-Michael; even the stars at night are part of their spectacle, and though we might briefly steal them away and rearrange them in our own scopings of horror, darkness and things to come, they remain the rulers of universe. The family displays its spoils: "the Queen sat there and drank a cup of tea *and also had a piece of cake* – very unusual *that!*" A photo of Joan Collins; *Tales of the Unexpected* was filmed here. And *The Lost Prince*.

I travelled briefly with the biographer of Stephen Poliakoff, *The Lost Prince's* writer and director. He was going to send me something and I have forgotten what it was; it never came. *Hidden City*, a film that inspires all my exploring, directed by Poliakoff, is still not available on dvd. I have not seen it for twenty years; appropriately, as it concerns a piece of forbidden film. Maybe it was a burned dvd copy of the movie that was to be sent.

Poliakoff seems to understand that what is generally and condescendingly scoffed at – secrecy, conspiracy and shame – are the working methods of The Powers; disciplines as mystical and esoteric as St Julian's, translated through squints. No wonder lords once hired hermits...

O my International Lettristes!
O my Situationists!

I FIRST CAME ACROSS the Situationists forty years ago, in a book by Richard Gombin called *The Origins Of Modern Leftism*. It had been given to my Dad by a local newspaper book reviewer in a pile of review copies. These were bound for sale at some church fête. I nabbed the Gombin book. In it I read something that has stayed with me ever since – a critique of everyday life:

> *"life in modern society could be reduced to survival (life brought down to the level of economic imperatives). Such societies are societies of the quantitive, the consumable... that is the only existence permitted... frenetic production of goods. Enrichment only results in an expansion of survival, leaving the quality of life untouched.... This applies across the board, including tourism, which imitates the circulation of goods with its 'package tours', its excursions lacking any element of surprise, its factitious recreations.... Life is thus experienced at one remove, it has become a show in which everything is becoming incorporated. This is the phenomenon to which the situationists refer as a spectacle... a merchant-showman economy, [in which] alienated production is supplemented by alienated consumption..."*

The idea that ours is a society of spectacle struck a powerful chord that is still ringing with me: a society in which the circulation and distribution of images defines social relationships subjugated to economic imperatives still seems to describe the one I 'operate' in.

The Situationists theorised tactics with which this spectacle might be disrupted and overthrown. The most important of these was détournement: the 'turning' of decrepit forms from their 'consumed' and 'consumable' functions into spanners in the works, grit in the eyes, flies in the ointment.

For the Situationists, art was dead, an irredeemable product and machine of the spectacle, its only usefulness being its capacity to be redeployed as a disruption of itself.

Détournement could be practised on the streets as well as at the printers. It could be triggered by going on dérives, walks that cut across all economic imperatives, in search of the emotional-spatial (they called it psychogeographic) information that would enable them to construct 'situations'; by which they meant exemplary events or behaviours that would prefigure and provoke the transformation of social relations to ones of propertyless creativity and unfettered mobility. (Like most of their tactics, the dérive was devised in the 1950s by the International Lettristes, one of the founding groups of the Situationist International.)

There was no geographical or economic destination for these dérives, they were not walks to a place of work, nor to the shops, nor to sites of pre-digested leisure, nor to places of religious worship. Instead, they were un-planned drifts, in which the criteria for choosing a route were: which promised the most abundant ambience? which had the greatest resonance, the greatest capacity to be détourned, re-deployed for the purposes of disrupting everyone else's economic trajectories? Most treasured were those places that seemed to manifest a meeting place of different ambiences. These were called "hubs".

These tactics struck personal chords for me, not dissimilar to my nights of youthful, experimental sexual adventures through neighbours' garden sheds and coal bunkers, expeditionary drifts across whole streets of back gardens, bike-catapulted dérives through Coventry council estates and trespasses into locked and shut-for-the-winter pleasure parks. But I can't think I'm even exemplary in this, let alone unique in such adolescent drifting. Most adolescents without liberal parents are surely forced to either suffer or dérive: without homes that we have control over, without full control of what we do in the bedrooms of our teens, we drift the streets or shrivel and burn. I suppose that, if there is any difference, it is that, in my middle age, I have once again responded to the erotic drive towards the streets and trespass.

The Situationists' walks, drifts, dérives were not ends in themselves. They were acts of research; experiences on the street were experimental materials for the creation of 'situations': combinations of site, performance and demonstration out of which might eventually spring new ways of living to transform cities. So, this is a walking that is not an end in itself, that does not test its own qualities in terms of how little its participants bother the public health service, but rather according to its coruscating engagements with the social relationships expressed in the images and ideas that circulate about sites and spaces. It is a walking of disruption, a walking of refusal, and a walking of research and redeployment of old arts in smithereens.

The conditions of these times are more restricted than those when the Situationists drifted Paris. While dictatorships are under threat since the Arab Spring, the supremacy of economic neo-liberalism has consumed all political oppositions in the overdeveloped world; the government-industrial complex barely bothers to conceal its exploitation of natural disasters and economic collapses to wipe its jaded slate clean and begin again from scratch – fishing communities flattened by tsunami and then unashamedly concreted over for holiday resorts and luxury flats. The Spectacle is now integrated, concentrated *and* diffuse: where once it operated through either dictatorship, free mobility, or the penetration of everything, now it deliriously switches, with alacrity, between all three states. In the overdeveloped world any resistance to the Spectacle has switched from the political realm to running battles across the plane of interiority. We are caught in a rearguard action to win back control of our own subjective multiplicities from identity-retailing and an avatar culture that proposes the arts as a tribute band and the streets as a lookalike competition; remember those zombies picked off by rifle fire from the rooftops in the turkey shoot from the *Dawn of the Dead* remake – that's us, that is. Under these conditions, and in this game of war for interiority and subjectivity, the tactics and, more importantly, the strategy of the Situationists have never been more resonant.

> *"the power of walking… its destructive ability to destroy the way we are meant to live in cities"* Will Self

…the unopened books in the library were bought for the look and feel of their covers. Three-metre tall polar bears rear up in death sporting their bullet holes. And I wonder if our looking for a narrative here is mistaken; and that, instead, this apparent jumble of absurdities and grandiosities is itself some strange heraldry that speaks not over our heads but straight through them. Leaving us with the feeling of having dreamed what we now believe. On the way here, wasps' nests in the roadside had looked like exposed human brains; last night in *Drive* a momentary glimpse of a head blown half away.

Lorraine emails me a few days later: "I think that something happened in Somerleyton. I came back looking at my journey home differently. I felt a bit like a detective. Or maybe more like that guy from the *Bourne Identity* films. I noticed it even in the way in which I recounted our day to my husband. Strange – but when I looked at one of your tactics about taking on the feeling or power of the shape you walk – it seems that somehow Somerleyton's lack of obvious centre left me seeking, searching one. I think this was encouraged further by running back to the train station. I seemed to see a lot of doors closing (car doors, front doors) or animals just scurrying out of sight. That feeling of 'something is hiding from me' stuck around for a few days. I even continued wearing my mac when it was not necessary. Nothing beats a sharp change of direction and the swish of the mac whilst walking."

I remind myself to send Lorraine some counter-tourism tactics to pass on to her sister for use in swish North Italian resorts. I am walking alone now, through Herringfleet, and it feels as if the ordeal of my walk is beginning. Meeting up with Lorraine, exploring the stately home together, playing at subtle intruders and mildly misbehaving tourists, egging each other on; we have shared a gentle subversion.

But now she is abruptly gone, running for her train, the suddenness of her departure is the disruption I need to get me started.

After pitting myself against the maze in the grounds, I still have some miles to walk...

Getting started

Five steps to the beginning of a great walk.

1/Knowing why

It is not a stroll in the park, but it does not have to be complicated, this walk for opening up the world. It can clear your eyes, peeling away layers of deception, spectacle and that strange "hiddeness in plain sight" that coats the everyday. But you will need to disrupt yourself, set yourself going and apart. You will need to shake up things for yourself, so that rather than wandering ankle deep through the sediment of discarded images and illusions, you kick them up and explore the whole whirling snowglobe.

2/Knowing where

You can drift anywhere. But to begin with, start in the familiar and head straightway off into the unknown. Remember, you do not have to get anywhere, there is no set destination. It is all about the journey. Generally, keep out of shops, museums, art galleries. Go to places you would not usually visit – courtrooms, waste tips, fairgrounds, industrial estates, morgues, stadia car parks, ornamental gardens, bad zoos. Avoid suburbia and countryside on a first drift. Slip down alleys, chase any intriguing detail; follow instincts not maps.

3/Knowing me, knowing you

While drifting alone is fine, you may find it best to start with at least one other person. Above six or seven and you will probably split into smaller groups along the way. Even if it was you who organised the meeting place and the time and maybe a starting idea, you do not have to be in charge. Let the group develop its own instincts and make its own discoveries. Drifts do not have guides or leaders. Remember, your focus is on the spaces you are passing through, let the focus shift from self and others for a while. Drift with friends, with friends of friends, with friends of friends of friends. The 'drifting group' should be a web of friendship and new acquaintance; but let that friendship be what you push off from – a drift will dissolve in chit-chat if you are not careful; as quickly as possible turn from yourselves to the terrain. You do not need to be a history buff or an architectural boffin to make mythogeographical walks. Indeed, experts may have to be tamed or distracted and prevented from turning drifts into guided tours. Any group of people will have different skills, stories and sensitivities that can be shared while teasing out the adventure and mythogeography of the journey.

4/Knowing how

You need to free yourselves both from your everyday and from your usual walking habits. Maybe start at a time that is odd for you – 3.45am, 9.55pm, noon... Make sure you have at least half a day. The drift is not a brief stroll (though later you may develop a skill for slipping in and out of a 'drifting mode'). Find a way to get you off your beaten tracks, and then off your off-your-beaten-tracks. If you are a hiker or mountain walker, then change your boots for trainers and walk suburbs and inner cities. Jump on any unfamiliar bus at random and jump off at the seventh stop. Order a cab, state a fare and ask the driver to drop you "somewhere anonymous", close your eyes until you arrive. Start with some kind of theme – maybe look for traces of rebellion, or for wormholes to distant places, for powerful symbols, for voids, or for where things are interwoven. If the drift diverts you onto another theme, that is fine. The drift may begin to unroll a story and you can look out for things that develop it. You might set out to collect things, or take things to leave as memorials or surprises, or you might plan to seek particular types of place: maybe the tops and bottoms of buildings, rooms without windows, memorials that have lost their purpose.

5/Knowing what

Sensible shoes, possibly – needs vary. Clothes to suit the season, unless discomfort is the burden you want to carry. Small torch. Some chalk. String for measuring fields of gunfire and lines of sight. Ribbon for unofficially reopening or renaming places. A small frame to capture images. Notebook and pen. Camera. Water. Something a little luxurious or unusual – an unpredictable treat for your companions, perhaps. Not maps usually. A small lump of clay. Avoid wearing sunglasses unless you have eye problems, leave the dulling of the world to others, instead cup your hands around your eyes to shut out the ambient light array and intensify the colours for a moment. You will notice what you miss on your first drift; take it on the second.

Après dérive: make some memento of your drift to share with your fellow drifters. Or show to others; they may become your next companions.

Disruption

What happens if we refuse to walk functionally? We will be late for meetings. We will arrive at our desks and counters and lathes quite unprepared and shocked by what we are supposed to be and do, quite ill-rehearsed for our roles.

Make walking a temporary disruption from your commute, from your exercise: you can return to those things later. You do not need to follow the injunctions of André Breton and Henry David Thoreau and make every break a final one. Be canny; learn how to disrupt yourself, then disrupt your disruption and return abruptly to the everyday.

Disruptions don't have to be massive, but when they are, like setting off into a wilderness, it is worth considering how to disrupt your radical disruption. When you return from a long walk, or even a brief but very intense wander, it is worth remembering that for those who have not been with you on the walk, it may be hard to connect to your experiences. Rather than batter everyone in earshot with this divide, better to share associations and reminiscences sparingly and perhaps only when your stories connect with the reflections of others.

...as I walk it is all the time a few inches from annihilation on a furiously busy, pavement-less road, repeatedly buffeted by the vehicles' displacements of air. Despite the huge front gates from Herringfleet to Saint Olave's Priory, I see no houses; if they exist they are out of sight beyond the curves of long drives. I pass a roadside floral tribute.

The organist's seat at St Margaret's Church in Herringfleet hovers precariously over the nave, a flimsy wooden chair set far beyond the edge of the balcony, as if supported by the body of air. In one of the windows of the church is a collage of salvaged fragments of stained glass, an abstract before its time; the broken body I am in danger of becoming. The patterns of coloured light thrown by the glass panels of saints are equally expressionistic; splashes of bloody viscera on pale stones.

Like the girl at 19 Magdalen Street, Saint Margaret was tortured for sex: scalded and burned by a Roman prelate who wanted her for his concubine. In her dungeon she had a dream: she was swallowed by the devil, who then split in two, and she, being released, awoke back in her dungeon. There she was beheaded by her 'admirer'.

I am walking through Viking settlements: Haddiscoe is "Heddr's Shogr" (sounding like a Lovecraft monster) or "Heddr's wood", Waveney is "troubled waters", Herringfleet , or "Herela – ing – flet", is "Herals's son's river's edge".

Nothing to do with herring. Or a fleet. The foundations of its church were dug with "local forced labour" (Rev. Dr. Edward C. Brooks, *A Thousand Years of Village History*). The Reverend Doctor suggests that the tower was first a secular watchtower and weapons store built to "discourage" the local peasantry, though from what he does not say, and later, possibly, a local treasury – another bank, then – before it became a church. At Hardwick House it had been the other way about: the bank built on the site of a Viking church erected at the end of the First Millennium.

At the ruins of St Olave's Priory, after enjoying the modern buttressing of the site, particularly the concrete pillars dated 1980, I cross to the riverside Bell Inn to drink two pints of Woodforde's Wherry. The bell in question was used by travellers to summon a ferryman from the opposite bank. On the pub's photoshopped, fuzzy cut-and-paste sign, a generic monk swings a bell, but is not summoning a ferry. The caryatid referred to by Rev. Dr. Brookes as being in the lounge bar I cannot find. Perhaps gathered up in a corralling of heritage. I check in to my B&B at Decoy Barn, and then, in the dusk, I skulk about in Saint Edmund's Church, Fritton, unable to explain to myself why I am repeatedly visiting ecclesiastical buildings.

Despite the failing light, I can still just about make out the recovered curling patterns that would once have covered much of the interior of the mediaeval building. The church then would have been alive with these shapes, like the town taken over by spirals in Junji Ito's *Uzumaki* manga, spinning worshippers into a mystical whirl.

Two plain iron rings are sunk into the arch of the apse; once used to hang a Lenten veil to obscure the altar during the dark times, another kind of Mist.

At the bar of the Decoy Tavern, a man begins a joke about three rabbis, but abandons it in favour of a quiet row with his companion about sensory deprivation: "When I look at you, the whole of my perception, touch, sight... that's reality... it's a dimension, you're in a dimension... it's the old Japanese idea... some people say there's no such thing as 'alien', but there's nothing else!"

Opposite the Decoy Barn B&B stands The Mad House, in its yard a large pile of broken bricks and a US military vehicle decorated with a Maltese cross keep company.

Saint Olave, King of Norway and converter of souls at the point of a sword, had a motto: "baptism or death!"

30.9.11

I have caught 'a chill' and shiver through the night, waking early. After my shower, tiny droplets of perspiration collect on the hairs of my arms. I had not planned for it, but I have dressed all in black today; a shadow of myself. Everything here being 'Decoy', I have a sense of being caught up in a diversion from a real Barn I should be staying at and from a real Tavern I should be drinking in. The actual places may be very close, but very slightly to the side of their copies, and I am just offstage, in the wings of what is real. I rather enjoy the staging.

A 'decoy', Paul, my landlord, explains, is a huge net with a mouth, placed over a pond or waterway, into which ducks are lured or chased; the net narrows to a point where the ducks are trapped, taken out and killed. "And put on the train to London, built with Peto's money." The red brick of the old Liverpool Street Station, Paul says, is Norfolk red brick. A wormhole.

There are poached duck eggs for breakfast. I write in the Visitors' Book, remembering one at a weapons factory in Zaporozhe; the previous entry being warm words from the Mayor of Birmingham; below these I wrote something like "weapons workers of the world, you have nothing to lose but your triggers" and signed it "Leon Trotsky". Nobody noticed, or nobody cared. Inside the factory huge blocks of semi-molten steel had raced down gullies barely beneath our feet and were cut into crude shapes by a machine monster, "STALINA, 1953" painted on its side. Overwhelmed by the heat, I asked one of the workers about safety and he replied: "Every day I go to work as if I went to war. The workers in this factory are allowed to retire at fifty." "Yes", whispered the translator, "and they die at fifty-one".

Today I am due to walk to Lowestoft, past the prison at Blundeston. Sebald's portrait of Lowestoft is demonological: a quarter of its population illiterate, streets with every other house up for sale, and today I will be visiting it during the biggest economic collapse since the 1930s; a finishing school in shock capitalism for the masses...

Scratching from start

AN IMPORTANT QUALITY OF THIS WALKING is its anachronistic pace, decelerated even for walking. Rather than the routine shocks of the montage of everyday life, it is, once the walker is in the zone, an extended slow tracking shot through life. At a gentle pace, at the mercy of the material world, a walker can put two and three together with ease; she can surmise, postulate, ponder, consider, forget and remember in the same train of thought, her brain bobbing along on the top of her spine, a wobbling watch tower, full of tools for discouraging uppity ruling ideas, wary of their esoteric symbols, their exoteric chaos and their directorial use of the jump-cut (the boat home diverted to the trenches, a life suddenly cut short by a sniper or a juggernaut). Only in such slo-mo walking can she easily and regularly stop to stare obsessively at details, lichen, ironies.

...not long after setting out, I am carefully studying a bare noticeboard on the edge of woods, claimed by mould, and thinking of my Facebook friend Simon Park in hospital with an inflammation of the heart, his body invaded by the very bacteria with which he makes his art. They have taken him for their medium this time, as he once encouraged organisms to use my *Mythogeography* book: the slime mould, pleasingly, explored the book and then promptly turned their collective back on it and set off, out of the Petri dish, on their own dérive. Slime mould understand mythogeography. They recognise its amoebozoan politics, so lobopodian...

Mythogeography

MYTHOGEOGRAPHY IS AN EXPERIMENTAL approach to places as if they were sites for performances, crime scenes or amateur excavations (let's say, grave robbing) of multiple layers of treasure. To get at these different aspects of place and space, mythogeography draws on all kinds of 'low theory'; amateur and poetic assembling into manifestos of things I have learned (mostly from others) while out on the road.

Mythogeography is a hybrid of ideas, tactics and strategies. It embraces both respectable (academic, scientific, culturally validated) and non-respectable (Fortean, antiquarian, mystical, fictional) knowledges. It judges these first against their own criteria and then sets the different knowledges in orbit about each other, seeking to intuit their gravitational pulls upon each other. The rewards are many, but there are frustrations. For example, my trawls through oceans of esoteric literature for quirky gems have sometimes left me more incandescent than illuminated; too often a minor swerve from a predictable path is passed off as a grand journey of spiritual innovation. Illumination is most likely to be found where things are modest and everyday.

Mythogeography explores atmospheres and the effects of psychogeography, it joins in the Fortean procession of 'damned data', those anomalies that are not denied but marginalised by respectable sciences.

Mythogeography regards explorers, performers, activists and passers-by as sites; all as multiplicitous, unfinished and undefinable as the terrains they inhabit.

Mythogeography is not a finished model. It is a general approach which emphasises hybridity and multiplicity, but does not attempt to limit this to any single combination of elements or homogenous model of diversity. Since attempting a provisional summary of my understanding of this approach in *Mythogeography* (Triarchy Press, 2010) perhaps the biggest change of mind I have experienced has been around agency. In 2010 I tried to describe the kinds of groups in which people might best use this approach; what I have found since is that people best make their own connections and communications and that the job of mythogeography is to put itself out there and to trust in people's skills at making things happen if they really want them.

The origins of mythogeography are in the work of Wrights & Sites, a group of artists and performance-makers of which I am a member. We found ourselves increasingly working in sharply contested spaces, often jostling with other occupants of these sites who were keen to secure a single meaning for a place: commercial, historical or cultural. In response we developed different 'mythogeographical' approaches, learning and drawing from past and contemporary artists of site, including Fluxus, Mike Pearson, Tacita Dean and Fiona Templeton.

Perhaps all the connections that mythogeography can make will eventually turn out to be a collection of dead ends. Or perhaps this is the beginning of a mapping of patterns of symbols, punctuations, dynamic patterns and underground lakes of pleasure that drive places on; a kind of mapping that folks will come to take for granted – more materially descriptive of what energises a place than any story on the evening news.

Mythogeography can only ever be practised in the future. There can be no mythogeographers or Mythogeography Departments. Only people interested in experimenting. A useful archive of mythogeography would be a contradiction in terms; if it continues it will be by becoming something else.

...similarly, I want to make a counter-tourism that encourages even those people who take it up most enthusiastically to turn their backs on it and make their own. Leaderless resistance made up of single cells that in hard times congregate and fruit. Without origins, heritage-less, its spiral traditions curling like scrolls in St Edmund's out of a nothing at their tail.

This morning The Mist is back and emerging from it are various patterns into which to slide: dew-sparkled spiders' meshworks, farmers on tractors harrowing geometrical blueprints into the flesh of their fields, bacteria making patterns on

Simon Park's enflamed heart, the *Uzumaki* of St Edmund's still spinning in my head, a partly fallen gate that makes a shape like something Fernand Léger might have painted. The less 'I' am, the more slime mould-like I can be, escaping immobility. My shirt is soaked with dew and perspiration...

Jouissance

THE WALK CAN BRING YOU and your body into new connections through its aches, blisters, shivering and sweating, dehydration in intense heat, dizziness, pain, exhaustion, alienation, involuntary joy, inappropriate arousal, hearing what is usually unheard, bristling with fear, being desperate to piss and having nowhere to go, longing for a hiding place... there is little pleasure for most people in such discomforts in themselves (unless you are cultivating them as the status symbols of extreme walking); but what about:

The pain arrived at *by* pleasure?

The aching from the sheer enjoyment of the walk?

Soreness from the fierce rawness of the experiences?

Walking *through* the blister pain and out the other side into ease?

The rush when the fear subsides and relief floods in environmentally?

The touch of a companion upon the hyper-sensitised body that connects it to a great audience of intensities, to a fellowship of pilgrim bodies, to a shifting, rippling auditorium of little deaths, to a flayed stage of associations and nerves, to a welling outwards that merges with the meanders of future drifts and sensitises the road itself?

...now as I walk along a section of the Angles' Way and for a moment in the trees, alongside water, riding the falls and rises of temperature...

Environmentalism

I SEE THE TREE with tree eyes, I hold the stone with stone hands.
Touch is a dialogue.

> *"to feel the stone is to feel the stone's touch"*
>
> Christopher Tilley

...I feel my patterns meshing with far older ones. Then the path abruptly turns to follow the shape of a giant field and I am enclosed by the green concrete of immense industrial fields, punctuated by huge gates, long driveways and hidden manors. Perilous walking conditions again, lorries and cars at 60 and 70mph on narrow lanes without pavements, wings and wheel hubs a few inches from my fragile hands and thighs.

The land is inundated, a rural-Ballardian world; anywhere animals have burrowed they leave spoil heaps of sand. I am walking on prehistoric beaches, as I expected.

Yesterday, having read of the ghost girl at 19 Magdalen Street, as I walked past the house for the station, I was shocked to see in an upstairs window an eyeless face peeking out at me over the sill; someone had left a half-mask propped in the window. One of the guides at Somerleyton Hall had told us: "His Lordship assures me that there are no ghosts. I don't believe in ghosts as I was a scientist in my previous life."

Human civilisations are gigantic memento mori. No ghosts, no popular history; only reincarnated guides. Apparently the *Britain's Most Haunted* presenters sat where the Queen unusually ate cake and "terrified each other silly".

I walk into a community of prison guards and, further within, pass by a hidden community of prisoners. The children of the guards have excavated an intricate and extensive den of trenches and tunnels next to the jail perimeter. Yesterday, Lorraine talked of the remaining USAF air bases here, self-contained worlds with their own shops selling US produce. I pass a house called *Atlantis,* then another called *Dejavu.*

From beyond a fence comes the crackle and acrid smell of a bonfire. Few, very few pavements or verges, even in the residential areas: I am surprised at how unsafe I feel in such a flat landscape.

The ideological machine of prison communities and military bases is now an ideal model in my head. Feet gently blistering. Ash settling on my head and shoulders. Pilgrim. Penitente...

Pilgrimage

'CHANGING ONESELF ALONG THE WAY' seems to be the dominant theme in contemporary pilgrimage, with a diminishing role for destinations. Reducing sites and shrines to vague and mushy approximations; servicing a fluid commodity-thinking that passes for spirituality. The ease of much modern travel, taking the quickest route to a holy or holiday destination, seems to rob the journey of pilgrim quality. While to choose to take a more difficult one smacks of self-indulgence. What if you make a pilgrimage without a destination?

Maybe postmodern pilgrimage has no end-point, but rather is a search, or a re-search, for the possibility of such points (or their manifestation in other geometrical forms – perhaps as planes, perhaps as patterns). The pilgrimage, without an end-point, has no space for belief in the efficacy of completion; rather the pilgrim steps into the hyper-flows of the world without map, staff, route, scallop... having to reconstruct 'pilgrimage' while in the motion of it, consciously and openly going as a 'pilgrim' partly to discover how the world, how people, how oneself (selves), how the landscapes, how the divine might respond to that.

I am left curious and attracted to this 'pilgrimage' and wondering about its possibilities, where it might lead in terms of unexpected contacts and meetings, in a different kind of understanding of the relationship between place and meanings (everyday and metaphysical), of material space (symbol) and its relationship to 'what cannot be represented'. I wonder if the 'ghosts' of earlier pilgrim practices would rise up on such a walk. Would anachronisms be renewed, emptinesses filled?

Rather than 'discovering yourself' (which isn't there to be discovered, but to be made in multiple forms) or striving to drain again from what has already been visited and priced, we might instead seek new spaces for holiness, new pockets of anomalous subjectivity in worn out official shrines sucked dry by those who have come to take rather than add.

There is very little real 'wrong walking'; there is some element of pilgrimage in it all.

...the blue plastic bag on the roadside does not contain the expected human head, but is stuffed with other blue plastic bags. An old moat full of green water, a watchtower church across the fields; moats, walls, fences, surveillance.

Is HMP Blundeston full up with Twitter rioters?

I pass Copperfield Terrace and a house called 'Trot Wood' and remember that the Peggottys lived nearby on the Yarmouth coast and wonder where mine and Paul's adaption of *David Copperfield* is touring today – Germany, China, Costa Rica? – at this very moment, perhaps, enacting our dramaturgical geography of an unreal Yarmouth coast.

Gunton Hall Holiday Resort gives the unfortunate first impression of a prison-camp. In the blocks, all the windows are open, emitting powerful blasts of disinfectant. It is turnaround day. Reception is in Gunton Hall itself, decorated with reproductions of paintings of cute 'historical' children in velvet pants and photos of crude but orderly japes from the 1940s. A be-sashed 'Miss Gunton' tips a bucket of water over a lathered male victim.

Both at Reception and in the Pavilion Coffee Shop the staff are lovely. Friendly and helpful, they guide me on my way. I drink a latte on the terrace.

Beyond the resort, a huge funfair is closed and silent, its giant rides serpentine and coiled, massive secular versions of the scrolls in St Edmund's Church: maybe I should use such rides for prayer?

Dodgy

IN 2013, MY FIRST-YEAR theatre students took me on a 'mis-guided tour' in Plymouth. Along with a blindfold walk, the invitation to caress a full-sized body made of ice, a ghost ride in a lift, the transformation of the civic hall into an imaginary morgue and a whispered tour to a graffito made by Francis Drake, I was 'transported' into the past through the medium of a dodgems ride, made effective and actual by the students' recruitment of the ham-handed showman who swallowed my fists in his and in that moment sent me spiralling backwards. The students only hauled me back by getting me to eat a Time Out chocolate bar; and then they presented me with a handful of brochures of 'future events'. The students were shocked when I pointed out that they *had* given me my future: the top leaflet bore the face of my teenage daughter, a photographic self-portrait used for a theatre poster. Such fortuitous moments never seem to occur on badly prepared tours.

...I walk through one of the BBC's Breathing Places ("places to inspire and motivate you to create and care for nature-friendly green spaces where you live"). It feels as oppressive an ownership as "Home Office Property Keep Out"; I don't want to be environmentally rehabilitated, I don't want to be reintegrated back into BBC Nature, I like my prison. I pass Earth Lane.

On a verge I find packaging for replica Nazi military badges; the abiding fascination with the mass production of murder. Lars Von Trier's *Melancholia* is on release, 'overshadowed' by the director's comments about the Holocaust.

"Yes, Yes, Yes to British Pork": a banner outside a vegetable wholesalers. The Planet Melancholia on its collision course for earth.

All along the beach are concrete pill boxes. Watch posts. Gun emplacements without guns. A phone to contact the Coastguards is bereft of its mechanism. SLUTS 4 EVA. The beach is long and peopleless and filled with dread. In the far distance a huge wind turbine unwinds. Looking over my shoulder, coming the other way it could be

THEATRE ALIBI WITH EXETER NORTHCOTT THEATRE & OXFORD PLAYHOUSE

CURIOSITY SHOP

STEREO

A COVER VERSION OF CHARLES DICKENS' ORIGINAL BY DANIEL JAMIESON

LITTLE NELL

EXETER NORTHCOTT Friday 8 – Saturday 16 March
Box Office 01392 493 493   www.exeternorthcott.co.uk

something unspeakable from *Whistle and I'll Come To You*. I am Michael Hordern, ambushed by a piece of carpet on an invisible string. That's *my* heritage: a culture of stories and feelings, in blueish black and white, a white haired Doctor who could barely remember his lines and a piece of old carpet and some string.

On the way in to Lowestoft, at the top of the 'Score', I pass a pile of stones that every night moves by its own volition down to the water; going there to wash themselves. I recognise the doorway through which George Borrow rode his horse during a feud with Doctor Ray and when I ask the house's owner if he minds me taking a picture of the door he says: "of course not, it's part of the history of the town".

High Street Surgery, "the most easterly practice". This is the first town in England to see the sun come up each morning.

The Armada Post is a nondescript shaft of wood, ritually replaced every one hundred years. Careful reading of a shop front reveals a tattooist moonlighting as a unioniser for the GMB. I pass a county council building with a watchtower and I misread "Euronics Centre" as "Eugenics Centre". I am not convinced that "Star Supply Stores" supplies stars.

Passing a poster for a one-man show at the town's Marina Theatre tonight, *The Star Wars Trilogy*, I call at the box office and book a seat. Maybe the performance will give me some ideas for how to create a web or mesh from the thin shards of observation and experience that are accumulatively and incoherently lodging themselves under my skin.

The walk along the beach has been too short for me to find any kind of melancholy rhythm and now the town riddles me with scattergun details and amputated narratives. Worst of all, I like Lowestoft. It is not the wasteland described by Sebald, the wasteland in which it would have been simpler to 'spontaneously' discover my provisional narrative of dread to liberation. Instead, that counts for nothing in a vibrant, working-class seaside town; yes, the odd shop is empty, but there is a rowdy buzz on the street, speeded by the unseasonably hot weather. Children on the beach are throwing stones at each other. Fish and chips and ice cream on the prom. People are friendly, though one woman is thrown by my "good afternoon" and replies "Bournemouth Choir", I think, and a middle-aged woman I ask directions from has to be helped with distinguishing left from right.

The town carries the distinguishing marks of New Labour investment; the High Street is ornamented inarticulately with numerous tiles and plaques from a succession of uncoordinated public art projects. I eat in a charity cafe pushing healthy food. There are smart rising and falling fountains like the ones at Somerset House. All this may be good for Lowestoft, but it disrupts my melancholic narrative until I meet the desperate and angry souls, agitated and being reasoned with, outside The Drifter pub. A pint of Lettriste, please. And the puzzled and humiliated man arrested for shoplifting from Tesco's; "happens all the time" the cashier assures me. It is a scene almost identical to that in Manchester at the start of my Hurst walk, except this man is submissive, as if he expected it to end like this. On his way to Blundeston? Or are all the jails full?

I see a group of young men gathering at the end of a cul-de-sac, as if waiting to be collected for work, overhear a young woman: "I'll have a few drinks and then I've got to go to the job centre". Are there any jobs?

I see two grinding worlds sit side by side; the far-from-desperate enjoyment of those who are so far surviving the crisis, savouring the bonus of a heatwave across September and October, and those who have 'missed out', lost souls, boozed up, seeking a drifting oblivion. Beside a large obelisk for the dead, I daydream about painting all the cannons pointing out to sea in the colours of a USAF bomber division.

As I re-read Sebald on the annihilation of herring, two baby gulls scavenge from Styrofoam punnets. I watch the first sunlight in England fading, again and again turning mistakenly to greet an approaching stranger, thrown by the legion of lengthening shadows: "the disturbing thing about mirrors", writes Sebald "and also the act of copulation, is that they multiply the number of human beings". At Somerleyton Hall the guide had encouraged us to stand between facing mirrors in the Dining Room and contemplate the infinite number of our images; megalomaniac cloning. Next to the Ballistics building on Orford Ness was a "complex array of lights and mirrors that coordinated signalling and marked the bomb release time, called the 'field of mirrors'": I have switched books. At a local bookshop I have found an account of the Cold War Weapons Research at Orford Ness. A poem of Sir Andrew Motion's suggests that he thought this 'field of mirrors' had the power of long distance surveillance, "a field of mirrors learns to see clear beyond the Alps", getting it mixed up with the immense Cobra Mist backscatter radar further up the Ness. I laugh in shameful joy; knowing that the shadows on the prom think me just as grandiloquent and ill-informed of practical things. According to the book there is one abandoned structure on the Ness whose function has never been revealed; the accompanying photograph is of something similar to the large concrete 'rings' featured in John Keel's *Mothman* mythos and in *The Hunt For Zero Point* (Nazi anti-gravity flying saucers) by Nick Cook of *Jane's Directory*; all three look like over-symmetricalised prehistoric henges built of fridges. I long more and more to visit the Ness. I have one chance, if my knees hold out; the boat crossing to the shingle spit on only one day during my walk.

On the Ness, spark photography recorded the flight patterns and corresponding airflow of shrapnel fragments; patterns I add to the scrolls, spirals, carpet crosses, Léger shapes, curled fairground rides, remembered motions of a carpet on a piece of string, and so on.

On the promenade I find a scrolling pattern bathed by low yellow sunlight and reflected blue streaks. The effect is reminiscent of the stained glass colours in St Margaret's, Herringfleet, and I wonder about the CIA's funding of abstract expressionism. Are we really kept in check by patterns? I had been annoyed when a woman said she saw me "going the wrong way" in the maze at Somerleyton Hall, partly because it was a sort of telling off, but mostly because she had imposed a single meaning on the maze as if it were a test in repetition rather than an instrument for unsettling the pattern of things; all those corners and turns and turnings back for whirling the brain's fluids into a vortex, getting lost in order to find a new self, or, in the case of Lorraine's mother, love.

Unlike Sebald, who panicked in the maze, I could only deliver one disappointingly trivial error before getting out. I might have set myself too simple an ordeal.

I attend the one-man performance of *Star Wars* Episodes 4, 5 and 6; it is more a work of biblical exegesis than drama. The audience's experience is largely determined by the depth of their prior knowledge of, and commitment to, the films as self-evident representations of something meaningful.

On a wall at the Marina Theatre is the score (a few bars) of a fanfare written for a recent visit by the Royal Philharmonic Orchestra; along with the 'Sunrise Project' and the 'Fightback Trust', here is New Labour's Keynesian portion. But where is the structure, where is the meta myth of the whole show itself, rather than its sources? These questions apply just as much to the one-man show as to the post-ideological, small-time Keynesianism of New Labour.

The repetition of good works without any belief in one's own motivation? Only a zealot for pragmatism could enact such a profanation: to offer good things while taking away goodness itself. Like the jumble of the Somerleyton tour, there is not enough narrative in the town or the show. Sebald's task here was an easier one than mine; he made recession morbid. But I am stymied by the half-life of the town and its post-ideology-ideology; by reforms as patently thin as manuscript paper and porous as staves that are achingly dismal for all their brightness. It is not a wasteland that is disturbing this time, but the patina that passes itself off as diversity, the shallowness as access, the fraction as fulfilment. I cannot be a prophet here: "what are you going to land on? One quarter, three eighths?" I wander back to my B&B at a loss for how to tell the story of what is happening to me; it is not a story. There is no personified and superstructural 'dark side' to fight and no benign 'force' to harness.

Outside this evening's B&B, one of the guests, a middle-aged woman on her mobile, is trying to sort out some complication with her son's wedding next day.

1.10.11

I sleep well at my quiet B&B. Is Sebald's problem when confronting catastrophe – nuclear war, ecological devastation, depredation of species, Nazism – that he sees everything but the catastrophe of class? He is unaware of, or opposed to, the idea that there operates a system that always tends toward, and thrives upon, crisis; with its watchtower churches, and its jolly, drunken, sailors soused on the spirits of their leaders' marinated corpses. Instead, Sebald is super-sensitised to the surprise of tragedy. The East Lowestoft war memorial states that it is ordered by rank: explicit, unapologetic, the Spectacle was never about deception but reception. Some years ago the spirit medium Doris Stokes owned up to me that even death, 'the great leveller', cannot level class. At a séance in Edinburgh I challenged her on the question of equality in the afterlife. Was our passage through death an egalitarian one? Or would class differences survive? She demurred, I persisted, she admitted: the differences would persist beyond the grave.

Walk in the footsteps of others

'MENAGERIE THEATRE' WALKED POET John Clare's escape route from his asylum in Epping Forest to his home in Northborough; then made a play about their journey and his.

At the time of writing this book Bridget Sheridan was preparing to walk Le Chemin de la Liberté – a WW2 escape route from occupied France into Northern Spain – stitching, as she walked, a red thread representing the route onto silk, a material used for the escape maps carried by British aircrew.

Such walks are not equivalent to their originals, but interrogations of them and stepping off points for new walks. Like Heraclitus's river (rather more mutable than it is generally understood) the path is never walked the same way twice, *is* never the same way twice.

"walk between milieus"

...today, I get myself ready to walk into devastation; the loss of all the herrings, gull chicks starving in their nests. Office blocks are the new cliffs. Another breakfast cereal dispenser falls apart on me.

Today I will have to walk through the pain of blisters and sores. The seam of my jeans has rubbed off the top layer of flesh on the insides of my thighs; red raw this morning each step is teeth clenching.

From the kitchen comes the sharp crackle of frying breakfast. The landlord does not listen to my query about the qualities of the town, but lauds the walk down the coast. When I ask him again he confirms my impression of money spent. "Some good, some bad", he adds, and is keen to relate in great detail the manner in which the council first took out a set of traffic lights and then put them back in again.

I enjoy my breakfast, chatting with a man who is escaping from "troubles" in Saxmundham; he tells me that one day we will not be able to speak our minds for fear of the drugs gangs. I tell him that welfare states are the solution to drugs gangs as they were to brewers and distillers.

The man complains about Brussels and the fishing industry. I say there is a bottom line. There are no fish. The herring have gone. For twenty minutes or so we munch our way through the economic and political crises in Europe. But it is the drugs gangs he fears, and his voice betrays a present fear, not just of voicelessness one day, but now; we are acting in Harold Pinter's *The Birthday Party* and he is playing Stanley. I am a stage direction. Perhaps there is some connection I am not making, closer to something more important than anything I have to say. He almost scoots from the room, without a goodbye, when the couple from Essex enter; the man has been out drinking with his bridegroom son.

We talk about Lowestoft and its virtues and the couple favourably compare its friendliness to their county's: "if you look at someone it's 'what you fooking looking at?' They want to fight you." The man tells us of the £120 he spent on his son's stag night, starting at 5.30pm and ending at 3.40am, showing off his new teeth, laughing at the idea of porridge. Mrs H, the landlady, is ebullient. Sebald would have done better to stay here, inexpensively, rather than spend money on the faded glory of the now defunct Albion. O, Blake!

Rough and ready working class, tattooed, shaven headed, the two men I meet in the breakfast room are superannuated babies; one with a rural, the other with an urban, accent. Both open to a conversation that is more than banter; amenable, serious, thoughtful, capable of solving things. The wide range of our breakfast conversation – weddings, Putin, dystopia – presages a day of dialogue. I am due to walk with Ivan today.

I limp painfully to the shops, squelching through my blisters to some sort of accommodation with discomfort; but the rubbed flesh is different and I wonder how, with a horror eating away at the sensitive meat below the skin, I can possibly walk the ten miles to my next B&B, not counting the usual diversions and tangents.

I barely make the hundred yards to the general stores. Then, a miracle. Half a pot of Vaseline on each leg and I can feel nothing, nothing at all; now squelching at both the tops and bottom of my legs.

I sit on the promenade, middle-aged twins on bikes ride by, soft under-chins, the same saggy shape, until Ivan arrives. He is surprised by the breadth of this morning's breakfast table debate.

Ivan is familiar with the area; a student contemporary of mine, he long ago returned here to set up a touring theatre with a very deep and particular commitment to this region. It thrives, 29 years on. Ivan, however, is no great walker, so he is surprised by what we find, but also able to make multiple associations.

Walking through Kessingland we speak of Chris. Ivan has heard of his sudden death and I can tell him of the meeting of old friends to spend time together remembering him, gathered at Jacquetta's house in Hackney; of going to the Marshes to enact a little ceremony, a few words of remembering, a poem from Matthew, and a structure that we burned and that collapsed into a bent cross. Close friends in our twenties, I had not seen Chris for many years, but a few weeks before his death he passed a message through a mutual friend to say that he had found a tape of us singing a two-chord song we had written together: "only make love with your friends". I had not got back to him.

At Kessingland we turned inland but are twice disappointed until we find a small tea rooms open. I drink orange juice, Ivan coffee. Then we visit the Kessingland Arts and Heritage Centre located in a caravan behind the tea rooms.

I love these improvised museums; like the History Hut at Chudleigh Rocks where the ivy bursts through the roof and frames the exhibits. The Kessingland Arts and Heritage Centre has an effective layout. At first it seems to offer little more than a few nostalgic prints, and yet by moving deeper into the caravan, on one side opens up a children's area with shells and sand to touch and then a closed door welcomes further incursions to the curious with tantalising glimpses of an oar and other artefacts through an incomplete wall. There is no sign or invitation, but on prising open the door I find a jumble of everyday and official history; Rudyard Kipling and tins of toffee and a papier-mâché head of H. Rider Haggard. When I ask if I can photograph it, the man chatting with the curator announces himself as its maker.

More heads! There have been beheadings, the ghost half mask, the skull of Thomas Browne.

The head-maker explains the subtly different techniques used for Haggard's head and for that of the head of a fisherman, also stored in the back room. But I find these distinctions hard to follow. The man says that the plan was always to display a whole dummy fisherman, and he now shows me parts of it sat in a boat, but this venture has been temporarily abandoned due to the fisherman's legs being mislaid during the Heritage Centre's move from the building now used by the tea rooms, perhaps left in its loft. O surreal joy: fisherman's paper legs in the loft of a tea rooms. We are well into lilo, bacon slicer and forecourt territory...

Being ready

I⟶ IS ALL ABOUT BEING FLEXIBLE and ready. The walker can draw upon what among contemporary dancers and movement artists are almost banalities now: the prioritising, above technique, of flexibility and preparedness to accept affordances, to respond, to be open and raw to the moment. All the tactics and ideas here do not mean much without such readiness, such pre-expressivity, necessary for spontaneous reaction to what the road throws at you, which is mostly offers.

There is a paradox here: preparing to be spontaneous. Unsurprisingly, this is mostly a *via negativa*; the removal of blocks and inhibitions. It is also creative in a negative way; those blocks and inhibitions sometimes produce useful delays and deferrals. So, simplistic readiness is not enough; what a chosen walking requires is a sophisticated readiness that is strategic, able to translate the immediacy and specificity of the offer from the road to a moving space on a sliding plane of generality: in other words, little things connecting to big things, every brush with the road part of a big picture; a body in flux in co-creation with spaces that are always under construction.

Every time we enter a room or a forest, the walls or the trees bulge very gently towards us and we swell very slightly towards them. All masses attract. Walkers should be like martial artists, using the momentum of the 'enemy' (anything other than themselves) as their primary energy, living off others' supply lines.

In the end there are no rules, but "in the end" does not come around that often. Rules are temporary; susceptible to texture, switches of scale, the invasion of micro-worlds, the slithering of planes, vibrant things, dialogue, decaying of scripts, the collapse of abject public art, the holing of space, the traffic of hubs, voiding, indecision at *plaques tournantes*, voiding again, edging land, pseudo-rituals and the invention of modern traditions. Any, or all, of these can click in at any time. Such is the multiplicity of possibilities that there is no point in trying to learn protocols for every eventuality. All that will suffice is a general preparedness; a readiness to slide down between layers, relaxing into situations, snapping to sharp manipulations. It is something like movement artist Sandra Reeve's 'ecological body': "from a position of 'being among' rather than 'being central to'... they may experience their own system as an intrinsic part of a wider set of systems... rediscovering the flow of environment, rather than the environment as a succession of places". No one can fully mistress this; sometimes everyone's next best guess is all there is. No one is immune to missing a chance or freezing with fear or embarrassment (happens to me all the time), particularly those who "STAY CALM AND..." and those, like me, who are unjustifiably infuriated by them.

There is no justice and no guarantee. The inspired leap of a lazy drifter can leapfrog the assiduous student of Situationist texts, but there is no certainty things will go either way. And yet all my drifting suggests that good fortune favours the sensitive and non-institutionalised. Though be clear; I am playing with benign forces here. I make no claim for any special powers over fascists, authoritarians or sadists; I am far from sure that any of this is immune from manipulation and contortion. At best drifters make themselves invisible, of no interest to the world.

"Y gwyr yn erbyn y byd." ("Truth against the world.")

...on our way to Covehithe, by the lagoons and reedbeds of Benacre Broad, Ivan and I discuss wind turbines and electricity pylons. I like the look of both. Ivan does not, but he is enjoying the view of two wind turbines across the Broad, and wonders at this sudden appreciation of their beauty. I tell him that pylons are so called because they are the shape of pylon portals in the Ancient Egyptian underworld; the National Grid is a tracery of death across the country, the power of Ka racing down the wires. I tell him of the death of Roland Levinsky, Vice-Chancellor at Plymouth University, killed walking his dog on Christmas Day by current leaping from the power line of a fallen pylon.

Ivan talks of Arthur Ransome and George Orwell, both locals, and we discuss their secret service involvements. I tell Ivan how our theatre company unknowingly contrived to billet a former KGB head of station at Istanbul with a serving MI6 officer. Well, if people will keep these things secret, how are you supposed to know?

Ivan speculates on Ransome's response to *Animal Farm*: "you put in Stalin and Trotsky, but where is Lenin?"

Ivan is working on a piece about the Auxiliary Units for a 'What if...' play about what might have happened if the Nazis had invaded England. I first came across the largely unappreciated history of the Auxiliary Units when preparing a mis-guided tour for the small Dorset town of Beaminster. The place had its own covert local terrorist group ready to instigate havoc come a German invasion: torching cars to stop evacuation, garden sheds stocked full of explosives to destroy key bridges and railway tunnels. My question to Ivan is "why this show now?"; Ivan is exercised by the problem of coalitions.

Ivan believes that other citizens would have tried to stop the Units, in order to avoid reprisals from the Germans. Each of the Units comprised a small HQ staff and a number of heavily armed patrols of up to eight men apiece. All the members of these patrols *knew their landscape*. If invasion came the patrols would 'go to ground' for a while, until the enemy had fully overrun their area, only then would they begin to emerge and raise mayhem. "I chose patrol leaders from successful farmers and fruit growers, one a Master of Foxhounds, another a game warden, and encouraged them to nominate their own men." (Captain Andrew Croft) Friends and relatives as well as employers and employees constituted the teams: tight associations and coalitions. They operated under the guise of the Home Guard, "moving around at night without being seen or heard". They dug Operational Bases (OBs), underground sleeping and hiding areas, ventilated, built of timbers and corrugated iron. Each one supplied with a gallon jar of rum: the necessity of ecstasy, of altered states of consciousness, for the work of resistance. Sten guns, Thompson sub-machine guns, plastic explosives, snipers' rifles. *Experiment was encouraged* even after one unit set Leiston Common on fire.

The beaches we are walking today were considered likely invasion sites.

Ideal procedure was for no shots to be fired in anger (only explosions) and to take no losses; the Units understood the power of not fighting, of absence, of the army that melts away. The patrol members took a new look at their landscape to determine "which parts might be useful to the enemy"; the "farms, the streams and the woods which had been their playground could soon become their battleground" (Richard Webster); identifying attack and escape routes would have been routine for poachers if they were recruited.

Ivan says he, like me, has heard the Auxiliary Unit rumours: of assassination lists, often with unexpected names (local chiefs of police, and so on) and at the top of all the lists, of course, says Ivan, was the individual who put all the local units together in the first place, the one person who could, willingly or not, expose them all. The Auxiliary Units, with their model cell structure, have provided the blueprint for pretty much every terrorist organisation since. In some way they model ideal features of a drifting group, members of a convivial dérive, but there, I'm doing it again, prescribing...

Leaderless

"ONLY ONE IS A WANDERER. Two together are always going somewhere." *Vertigo* (1958), directed by Alfred Hitchcock, screenplay by Alec Coppel and Samuel Taylor.

This cuts to the heart of convivial drifting. For the shifting space of disrupted walking is one through which we *can* negotiate with each other all sorts of differences, helped by that quality in drifting which seems to favour the margins. The best things always seem to come from those on the fringes of a walking group, rather than from its head. *A fo ben, bid bont.* ("Who would be a leader, learn to be a bridge.") It is the tangent, the link, the scuttling off sideways, the 'crab walk' which heralds the best adventures.

It is always possible to directly share things; a burden, for example, that is passed around the group. This helps to shift power around the group.

There are no conventional guides or leaders on a drift. Someone may have set the whole thing up but they should feel no obligation to take control of the drift. If they have an idea for the drift – a theme, perhaps, like 'wormholes' – then they can introduce that to the group at the start of the wander, but it is always best to make clear that at any moment the drift could throw up a new and better theme, a different narrative, and everyone should feel free to follow that.

I have been on drifts where the group has split, perfectly amicably, to allow the different parts to pursue different things, or because not everyone is comfortable with taking a particular turn (say, into trespass).

In drifting the group composes the drift together, sharing, assembling, collating and collaging it. There are power issues in any group, but the constant to and fro of a good drift, in which the focus is switching all the time and the initiative moving from one person to another, together with the prioritising of 'and and and' over 'either/or', seems as likely as any other behaviour to diffuse and disperse the problem of 'leaders' and 'experts'; at best, new directions and ideas emerge before thinking and without it being clear from whom they came. If someone slips into a guiding role, then it's everyone else's responsibility to distract them from it.

There is another contributing factor to the dispersal of power that can develop in a drifting group and that is the peculiar sideways displacing of eroticism on good drifts. I cannot be certain, of course (I don't monitor the lives of my walking companions), but as far as I am aware, no romantic relationship has ever begun directly as a result of people meeting on dérives I have helped to organise. In the usual order of things, this strikes me as extremely odd. After all, drifts tend to 'throw people together' in intense shared experiences. I think the key element is that the primary focus of a good drift is the terrain, both outside and inside, so that desires shift from the fetishised, distinct and detached personalities of other walkers to a shared terrain of less familiar geo-erogenous zones that is already without and within. This is a prelude to the overthrow of Fatherland and Motherland in favour of Loverland.

Movement artist Sandra Reeve has described how she can 'guide' a student by her own movements: "aware of my own movement *in the environment* and then of the student's movement *as part of the environment*. As I move, I receive the atmosphere of the other mover through all my senses and then allow myself to respond to their 'landscape' through movement." I think something similar happens on the drift, through its heightened sensitivity to terrain, the "atmospheres" of the other drifters become psychogeographical, their erotic energies and physical attractiveness become expanding landscapes rather than fixed objects of desire.

I cannot remember ever being on a drift where there has been an open confrontation with someone about 'taking over'. Mostly there is gratitude to anyone who takes a moment to bring some special association or memory to bear upon a place or to share some knowledge or experience; and when the moment is over it is time for someone else to point the way, spot the appealing corner, draw everyone's attention to the hint of a reflection... and everyone else's responsibility to respond to that new impetus, adding to what has just come before.

(With thanks to Sergio DuBois, for asking the question.)

Nine pins

In Clive Austin's 2013 documentary about seven-dimensional walking, *The Great Walk*, the alchemical-walker Anton Vagus, a product of the 1960s walking revival, assembles a group of nine exemplary walkers for a 'fantasy drift' that lasts for years until one of their number disappears from the cliff tops at Berry Head in Devon while in the company of Vagus. To find out what happened next you will have to watch the movie. 'The Nine', though no longer together, can still serve as the model for a drifters' party game: choose the nine people – alive or dead, friends or strangers – who, at this moment, you would most like to join for a 'fantasy drift'.

Who are your nine?

...and why was the loyal service of the Auxiliary units never celebrated until very recently? Why were they told to "regard it as a matter of special pride" to never reveal their courage? Did the strategists think they might be needed again after the war? Against their own population? In the same way that parts of the similar Gladio network were deployed in post-war continental Europe? Or against invading Soviets? Shottisham had an auxiliary unit patrol. I am due to pass through that way later, where a person might plunge, like a Norwich bus, into a secret base beneath the fragile outer casing of the world, straight into the OB of the Underchalk...

Holey

THE UNDERCHALK IS A NOTION that circulates among some psychogeographers; that the English rural landscape is a fabrication, a thin surface held up on stilts and braces, through which one might tumble into a void.

...perhaps the post-war reticence about the Units' existence has something to do with their 'Special Duties', publicly described as information gathering; nothing has yet been said about what information was being gathered or what was to be done with it.

We speculate on what the feelings of soldiers seeing invaders emerging boat by boat from The Mist might be; German soldiers on a Normandy beach or Allied ones facing a 'what if?' Operation Sea Lion.

Sebald imagined the Dutch Fleet off Southwold in 1672. Ivan imagines a radical escaped from Manchester, a Communist perhaps, arriving in East Anglia, trying to explain to the locals that those trains arriving from the North West for the Harwich Ferry are not carrying cattle, but Jews from Cheetham Hill. How would the East Anglians have responded? Uprisings and insurgencies are rarely inspired by direct personal interests, but often by sudden irrational, often short-lived, identifications and empathies, hence the difficulty of predicting revolution, even by those making it: the denial of minority rights in Timisoara, restrictions on male visitors to female student quarters in Paris, the overturning of a market cart in Sidi Bouzid, a poetic play in Riga.

As we discuss these things we walk a dread, terrorised landscape from which blackened trees rise up from the shallows, tentacle spider-monsters loom up where eroding orange-brown 'cliffs' subside, silver birch trees are crashing onto the beaches ahead, and a single tree trunk, inundated, dead but still standing, wags like an ecological finger.

Elegant, horrific, dead, salted, assaulted by waves, prophetic remnant. One of the stripped trees comes on like Louise Bourgeois's *Mother*.

We face our own terror without any sublimeness; foolishly taking a risk we should not, the kind we would be furious if our children took, we set off to beat the incoming tide along a narrow strip of mud at the foot of the Covehithe Cliffs. We slide and scramble uncomfortably over slippery plateaus, the path up ahead obscured, until, after a quarter of an hour of anxious clambering we safely make a larger area of beach and walk on, distracted, missing our turn off the beach.

Rather than retrace our steps, we cut back through the fields to Covehithe Church, passing a map with one of those 'You Are Here' marks, except that on this map 'Here' has been rubbed blank by the tips of numerous self-locating forefingers. As if placing oneself in this landscape is to disappear the very 'Here' you are.

We pass a bird hide and I recall *The Hide*, filmed locally, and its twist: which one of us is the ordinary-seeming psychopath, which his sinister-seeming victim?

The seventeenth century church of St Andrew sits within the elegant ruins of the far larger mediaeval edifice that it replaced and cannibalised. The larger church, the unsustainable vanity project of its architect-priest, was transformed into the building needed by the small local community; leaving a ruined and wonderful frame.

This is one of those moments of qualitative change in a walk, for what the church is giving me right now is a tactic that I will be able to use at any scale – redeploying something (a place, an object, a philosophy) to create a model of itself within its own ruins.

This is also a utopian space, because I am now sitting in the sun within the ruined whale-skeleton of the mediaeval church and imagining doing this to the Gherkin, to the Palace of Westminster, to Buckingham Palace, making tiny models from their ruins so everyone gets the chance to be a high-flyer, a legislator, a royal.

I just remembered: somewhere at home I have one of the fragments of a photograph taken by the artist Richard Long on one of his epic walks and cut up by its owner, Bill Drummond, into 20,000 pieces...

Tactics and things

IN ONE SENSE, tactics are never anything much more than 'catapults': like the taxi suggestion in **Getting Started**. They provide you with a beginning; everything after that is provisional, something worked out between you and everything else.

Covehithe Church gave me a new tactic. Here are some others that arose from particular places or things; all of them can be applied beyond their immediate place of birth, at varying scales, and with variably unpredictable consequences.

⊤ Talismans

Carry ephemera in your pockets; talismans of popular memory. Plastic daleks and so on. Carry cheap trinkets for leaving in empty niches. Place dear memories in cracks and on empty rock shelves; return in a year or so to find out what has happened to your associations.

⊤ Make poems from house names

Heejee

Cults

Didjabringabeer

⊤ Burden

The performance artist He Yun Chang picked up a rock on the beach at Boulmer in Northumberland and carried it on a route roughly around the coastline of the UK. He wanted to set himself the arduous task of carrying a rock around an island and Manhattan was too small. I joined him for a short while. He paid little attention to the terrain he walked through, other than collecting fallen apples. His focus was on his task; his rock was no pebble.

Explore the recalcitrance, resistance and resilience of objects. Set them against your walking.

Carry your own walls, gates, fences, bollards, tripwires, mantraps, pits, razorwire, 'no entry' signs.

When Simon Whitehead walked through rural lanes with a table on his back he brought the homely into the outside and turned it upside down. There is a wonderful photo of Simon with the table. I have seen it shown in presentations (and I have it in Simon's fabulous book *Walking To Work*). After multiple viewings, certain things have begun to strike me about it: Simon did not take it (obvious, really), there is a community in the distance, there is a coast, a power or telephone line passes overhead, barbed wire runs along the tops of the hedges, the image is constructed so that the road disappears into mystery, one that Simon has emerged from... it is less romantic than it at first appears, and as well as representing Simon's action there are other vibrant things in motion in it; representation, condensation, imprint.

⊤ Haul

Lonnie van Brummelen dragged a sculpture of Hermes for three months along the sides of roads. By the time she reached her destination, Hermes had mostly 'dematerialised'.

Choose something to drag; something that will leave a mark, something that transfigures as it is pulled.

I witnessed a comparable dispersal of sculpture, similarly neo-classical; a cheap piece of garden sculpture appeared in pieces at the bottom of an alley near the main railway station in my city. Its various broken parts moved around the lane for some weeks and I began to photograph them; they moved on their own, they moved with the most desultory forms of human and animal assistance. The final piece hung about for months and then one day it was gone for good.

⊤ By the yard

Take tiny walks while thinking of very long ones. Merlin Coverley recounts how the Nazi war criminal Albert Speer walked 'around the world' while pacing a prison yard over the years of his sentence, recording each day's imagined journey in his diary; still an imperialist in his years-long daydream. Examine the routes your imagination takes, for you may find that the terrain is as ideological as it is fantastical.

⊤ Two heads...

Take a small piece of modelling clay, shape it into a representation of your head and then keep it in your hand or pocket on your next drift. That way you always get to see things from more than one point of view. I got this idea from Saint Nectan who picked up his decapitated head and carried it home to his hermit shed. And where his blood fell foxgloves grew. The sight of foxgloves is always an extra prompt to multiple-seeing for me.

> *"A transient mountain... just passing through... moving at the speed our fingernails grow."*
> Doreen Massey about Skiddaw Peak

╦ You are (not) listening to....

Use a smart phone, a discreet earpiece and an internet connection to the website 'You are listening to...' (**http://youarelistening.to**) in order to access the displaced commentary emerging from the emergency services of giant cities. The voices of deadpan despatch workers are set against bland lounge music.

Eavesdrop on fires and murders, on the slowly unfolding urban warzone.

Combine this disparity, which presents itself absurdly as a seamless everywhere, with the disjunctions upon disjunctions that will present themselves to you as you walk with this obscenity in your ears in Dnipropretovsk, Linares, Basra, Baginton, Xia He...

...then, maybe, after a while, drop the things and the places...

╦ Punchdrunk

Walk in masks.

╦ Gnostic walking

Walk disembodied, walk out of your body.

The walk itself and the terrain for it are both equally irrelevant to this walk; all that is important is a small divine spark inside to which you should give your full attention. Let that spark grow until it consumes your walking body, the walk itself and the world walked in. Walk embodied and disembodied simultaneously; first shifting from one to the other until the walk becomes pure shift. Walk as smoke. Then, when you are ready, walk out of your skin and into a suit of worldflesh awaiting you in the suite of connections; walk not.

...I am becoming increasingly suspicious of Sebald's exploration. I had assumed that *The Rings of Saturn* proposed itself as a deep engagement with its landscape; those who had recommended it to me thought so. How ironical is it meant to be? Perhaps there was no engagement? Or is there a mismatch between Sebald's complex intellectualism and his idea of what an embodied engagement with a landscape is. He does not match up to Nick Papadimitriou's 'deep topography'. Increasingly, parts of *The Rings of Saturn* are re-reading to me like cursory desk-based research....

Deep topography

THE CLASSIC ARTICULATION OF NICK Papadimitriou's 'deep topography' comes in his seminal *Scarp* (2012), an account of his journeys to contain in his words and sweat a "vast and yet seemingly invisible presence... hover[ing] over the northern suburbs of London". Subjecting himself to the North Middlesex/South Hertfordshire escarpment, Papadimitriou's becomes a body that can "become the stratum of gravels surfacing on a hill track after heavy rain". Curling inside his looping journeys, Papadimitriou de-romanticises ruins and tweaks the erogenous zones of golf courses. Other narratives bend like tiny dimensions inside the bigger shell, while mythic figures step sure-footedly around his own wanders, such as Gloria Geddes: a disappointed goddess, contemplating the railway tracks, terminally betrayed. Nick Papadimitriou calls this wandering and watching and logging and obsessing "deep topography": the repeated walking of the same stretch of terrain, observing and re-observing, reading and researching, deep in information and feeling, the terrain and the body seeping into each other, the map into the mind, the mind into the map.

...Ivan says he skipped chunks of *The Rings of Saturn*. I have been more diligent, but equally baffled as to why passages extolled as perfect prose mimic the clutter of local history pamphlets. Is Max Sebald really engaging or racing through as he makes a few notes? Or not much concerned with the terrain; a Cartesian mind musing above the fray.

Sebald's conversation with the gardener at Somerleyton Hall has the same contrived convenience as the *Down Your Way* 'encounters' of Nicholas Crane's *Two Degrees West: An English Journey*. I think I have misunderstood him. Mistaking the connections and coincidences he weaves as sections of loops that return to their trajectories further along the path. But Sebald's work is not about returning to the path; he is a flâneur not a dériviste.

I doubt if the quotidian wonders of this terrain would be of much interest to Max; the 'grotto' behind the door of the Kessingland Arts and Heritage Centre caravan. Did he find places like that, but edited them out?

There's a bees' nest in Covehithe Church, rumbling like bombers. Earlier, on the beach, Ivan mentioned a hum he could hear. I could not. There are grapes on offer in the cool church and I guzzle many; ripping their flesh with my teeth, they explode like sweet puri coating my throat with their juice. I drop some coins in the honesty box.

The long, very straight road we walk down, running inland from Covehithe Church, is called Air Station Road; off it runs Cut Throat Lane. Such clumsy hints at extreme local histories, though generic, often contain handfuls of empirical, localist gems; accidental id, like sourcing from 'true crime' books. In the fields, huge sows are suckling hoards of piglets. A giant boar is mounting a sow. Life grunts on.

Walking the ascetic concrete paths through a pig farm, Ivan is reminded of the pig-man in *O Lucky Man!*, a mad experiment; perhaps he escaped. Or became us. There is an affect in this landscape: it seems to shrink back from us, it feels rather than perceives or performs, sniffing scandal and poison, meat at the industrial scale, interference at the cellular level. The coming of fire.

In the pig field we spot what looks like a partly excavated classical bust and I tell Ivan about a skull found and secretly buried in a concrete wall on Orford Ness to avoid a disruption to the building of the laboratories. The dusty soil has been churned by the pigs, then dried by the sun in model mountain ranges that remind me of the miniature desert landscapes I explored at ankle level, a child in my Dad's gardening patch…

Autotopography

I HAVE SOMETIMES WONDERED whether there is in my personal history some explanation for my attraction to a very ordinary exploratory walking.

I got lost in Channock Chase with my cousin; we tried for hours to find our way back to our parents in the giant, silent, unreplying forest.

One year I spent the hot summer days listening to Radio Three while pushing toy tanks through a dry, crumbling clay-red terrain that rose up in clouds of ochre dust under my model barrages. With my head to the soil the dry lumps of my Dad's vegetable plot turned into the eroded mountains of a desert somewhere just to the side of Nevada.

At the age of 15, I ran errands – walked errands, really – in the building society where my Mum was employed as a cashier all her working life. I earned four pounds and nineteen shillings for my first forty hour week.

I do not associate walking with leisure. I was never a rambler. The boots I first walked in disruptedly were not hiking boots. They were working boots; I was issued them when I worked for Continental Landscapes, a division of a Dutch-owned multi-national firm with a contract to maintain the grass verges on council estates. For those nine months I would either be walking behind a Hayter, a big grass cutting machine, dangerous enough to snap the fingers of one of my colleagues and back her up against a fence before we could turn it off, or wielding an industrial strimmer that flicked slow worms in two and dog shit in splats onto your mask. All the time, walking, walking… so, more than leisure, walking is just as likely to make me think of work.

On a school trip, walking across an air strip on the top of the Long Mynd in Shropshire, I happened to glance over my shoulder to see a few yards away a glider silently bearing down on me.

I was Coventry Schools' race walking champion at 15. I won because I could turn races into melodramas, always ending with a final burst of speed for the line. I remember the adrenalin rush, the absence of any weariness for those hallucinatory seconds. One race I went too early, taking the 'frontrunners' with me and the first five of us collapsed on the track in sight of the finishing line. We made the main headline story on the sports pages of the local paper for that. I can't remember the victories, but I remember the jouissance of that losing. Give me altered consciousness over competition every time.

Until I was three, I lived on a busy road in Coventry, the Foleshill Road, next to the Courtaulds factory and a working canal. When I was about 11 months old, before I could stand on my own, I used a teddy bear to climb out of my cot, splitting my lip in the fall, and made my way down the stairs, through my Nan's shop, out the shop entrance, and headed up the Foleshill Road on my hands and knees. I was spotted by the woman who ran the sweet shop on the corner, who ran out and rescued me. When I was three we moved

to a smarter edge of town on the cusp of the rural. I walked to school through a spinney. Over the years, in that spinney, I would meet up with girls, slide on frozen ponds, gaze into the big warm windows of a detached house and wonder if the Antichrist lived there, discover a huge cache of porn mags wrapped in newspaper under the leaves; it was there I would be hurling a stick to bring down conkers when our car pulled up and I was told my Grandad Smith was dead.

I remember my adolescent dérives, drifting on bikes between the council estates and big houses of suburban Coventry, switching gnomes from garden to garden, treating the night-time suburbs as our own movie set. My geography is not only public, but also private. I am as concerned with the shells of Bachelard as with the empty spaces of de Chirico.

On tour at the Leningrad State Comedy Theatre in 1990, I walked in the interval in a wooden-floored room at the Kirov Opera (it was *The Queen Of Spades*; Pushkin coming alive, I recognised the sets onstage as places in St Petersburg, then Leningrad, that I had been walking during the day), promenading with our drinks in a clockwise direction around a bust of Kirov: murdered by Stalin for being too St Petersburg and not Moscow enough. Next day I walked obsessively up and down the Nevsky Prospect, dreaming I was a character from Andrei Bely's Symbolist novel of the city, *Petersburg*:

> "*Contemplating the flowing silhouettes Apollon Apollonovich likened them to shining dots. One of these dots broke loose from its orbit and hurtled at him with dizzying speed, taking the form of an immense crimson sphere...*"

I have been on many political marches. Most were dull affairs, but marching in a Bloody Sunday march next to an INLA pipe band taught me something about the terrifying power of walking to a beat, whilst in Dresden in 1989, a week after the Berlin Wall fell, but with the Stalinist Government of Honneker still in power, marching was scary and hilarious at the same time. I never heard so much laughter on a march. Less than two years later, on a spontaneous Anti-Poll Tax march in Bristol with a few thousand others I experienced the wisdom of the mob. Approaching the Council House where a meeting setting the local Poll Tax was in progress, the police lined up a wide swathe of horses across the road in front of us. Those of us at the front slowed the march to a crawl, struggling to think of a next move... Suddenly there was a murmur behind us and people started to break off from the march and race down a side road. At first we tried to stop the breakaway: "stick together!". But the crowd *knew the landscape*, pouring through a back way to the Council House. Seeing the move, some of the police riders split away to cut off the breakaway marchers; before they could close ranks we had marched straight through the gaps and onto the Council House green, police horses milling in our wake: the collective wisdom of a leaderless mob on the move.

The walking I do now is different from the walking in those memories. And at the same time it is influenced by each one of them.

Perhaps it is because I come from families of engineers, glassblowers, cashiers, servants, butchers, pattern-makers, slaughtermen, snipers and Cold War fighter pilots that I have so little sentiment for a fixed location in the land and a distinctly unromantic sense of the industrialised countryside. Because my people have always gone where the industries, the big houses and the big armies have gone. If you want to go back 300 years we were water gypsies on one side and, on the other, gentlemen farmers, lords landless who never owned but always rented their land. When contractors demolished our mansion-like farmhouse in the 1940s (vacated by our bankrupted family a century before) they found a room without doors or windows, a secret room; even when we were comfortably wealthy we were never 'at home' in our home... is this why I am resistant to any suggestion of completion in place? Why I am always ready to walk?

> *"If we are to remember much material we must equip ourselves with a large number of places. It is essential that the places should form a series and must be remembered in their order, so that we can start from any locus in the series and move either backwards or forwards from it."*   Francis A. Yates

...later that evening, I walk alone from my B&B at Poplar Hall back to the Five Bells Inn at Wrentham. It is my second visit of the day, Ivan and I having stopped there for a couple of pints on our way in; always a sign of weariness when I repeat a route. It is a slightly unnerving walk through a silent wood, then the *O Lucky Man!* pigfield and a treacherous track.

Mist rises. I see the road ahead, but the road turns to Mist too and just looks 'wrong'. I have come a bad way and I have left the map behind at the B&B. I turn back, then turn around again and carry on, I keep walking and find I have been thinking ahead of myself, fooled by a concrete drive to a water treatment plant. I still have 200 yards to go before my turn. The place is trying to trick me now; I have fallen for it, become infatuated with it already. So soon into the walk, imitating a loved one. Blistered feet on rocky shards; love it and hate it, jouissance, my old friend, the more you hurt me the more pleasure comes to me from everywhere.

I am being watched by something. Eyes in the trees. The big ruined windows of Covehithe Church were full of blue. I have blue eyes, a sky framed by a body of ruin wandering around a maze so large it threatens to swallow species. The Mist leaves a shiny dampness on my shirt and coat.

The print by my pub table is 'The Death': a Leicestershire hunting scene. Fake heritage; why, what other is there? It had not really struck me until today that it is the North Sea I am walking with; the extent and power of it, and this vulnerable, low lying land, so devastated in 1953. Even on a day like today, with barely a wave, Ivan and I spooked ourselves under the cliffs. In place of the fucking couple observed by Sebald below those Covehithe cliffs we saw a pig mounting a sow. Why was Sebald so distressed by his encounter? Was it seeing orgasm from the outside, the interior exteriorised, like a head suddenly opened up or blown apart, or seeing the space between people annihilated to nothing? While we were on the beach I forgot all about this incident from the book and it only returns to me now as I sit in the pub and nurse my memories of the day, prompted by the arrival at the next table of a young couple who wrap their attentions around each other; Ivan had pointed out some debris and we had talked of that, of places where people could come to be remote and unmolested, *unregarded*, to do things which while not harmful were best enjoyed in some kind of remote and airy privacy. It was there, where we had felt our mortality, that Sebald said he had seen the mollusc-like couple.

A window is keeping a watch on me. *Whistle and I'll Come To You.* Whistle. Please.

Anna at Poplar Hall says otters have cleared their pond of fish, big carp and all. I thought of Nic Green waking beside the river. Ivan says Suffolk has big estuaries, but its rivers would barely be called streams elsewhere.

2.10.11

Last night I caught a taxi back from The Five Bells. The Mist had come down and I did not fancy walking narrow unlit lanes in black clothes without a torch. The Mist at times made a ceiling just above the car, as if we were driving through a narrow tunnel. At Gunton Hall, Machen's cloud of sparks took real form in the photo of a Zeppelin attack. The sky is a secret tunnel.

I am not far from Leiston now, I have an address for my grandfather there; known as 'Little Moscow' for electing a Communist Party Councillor, Ivan said, implying that this was due to some technical error in the electoral process, but last night I read that there was a significant Communist movement in the town.

Poplar Hall, my B&B in Frostendham Corner, was empty before the Second World War; renovated to re-house one of the farming families whose lands were requisitioned for one of the US air bases just to the South of here. At the Lowestoft B&B the anxious man told me he was the fruit of the Cuban Missile Crisis, his mother told him "people took comfort in each other's arms". I am disproportionately embarrassed when the entangled couple from The Five Bells come down to the breakfast room and take up a table that puts us in the same relation to each other as at the Inn; I decide against conversation. The locally smoked haddock at breakfast is stunningly well done.

Such hyper-sensitisations make revelation a modus vivendi, a default, a habit. Distinct pleasures to be sought not for snobbery or greed, but for the sake of our senses; these are the means for making a body an open laboratory for accidents to experiment on.

At South Cove I find a graveyard collection box, shaped like a church with a huge padlock on its nave; "mind-forg'd manacles" again...

Cemetery Walk (2003)

I OFTEN WALKED WITH MY WALKMAN on. Not when drifting, but when I had a destination to get to. When I wanted to be there already. The effect of the music – this may have had something to do with the kind of music I listened to – was to coat everything around me with a thin film of cinema. I blocked out the diegetic sounds of places I passed through, often reading as I walked, crossing roads without realising… but sometimes, even with the Walkman on, perhaps because of the music, I began to drift.

I'd just walked for an hour through the town of Basingstoke, to see the movie *The Mothman Prophesies* in a public toilet of a studio in a Warner Brothers cinema complex on the edge of the town. On my way there I had been impressed by the apparent anonymity of the town, its humourlessness, its lack of anomaly. The only thing that caught my eye was a burnt Stars and Stripes flag. I found its distressed synthetic form hanging on a traffic sign.

I pocketed it. But it didn't raise my spirits. On the way back I put on the Walkman again. I was just as miserable as before, and weary now at the prospect of another hour of walking. And, then, just as it is so often on dérives, just when you are tiring, just as you have to make an effort to walk at all, you begin to drift:

> I suddenly just turned off, into a cemetery… on a whim. As I turned off the tedious artery and into that Basingstoke cemetery, I wasn't really sure why. There was an odd heraldic badge on the iron gates, and in the distance there was a black car that seemed to be moving, but not getting any closer. There was some promise of ambience. I went in. I started to read the gravestones. I was listening on my Walkman to *War Of The Worlds* (the Toddy Terry remix). I was immediately struck by the brutal, crude, vulgar power of the feelings expressed ungrammatically – soon I was weeping absurd tears – the effect of unsophisticated, unpunctuated ornamental masonry.

> For All
> Our Babies

> Always Loved
> Never Forgotten

> The locked chapel. The black doors.

Fallen headstone
An urn
Snapped off at the stem

A cross with an unnatural arm of ivy

Pricked by holly... feeling alive

The black car ahead
Still – not getting any closer

The red lights
On the roof

It's already darker in here

Full up with piss and beer
On the fence

The car with red lights has gone
Suddenly

The dearly loved child
Called to rest

Can't help thinking of my own children

No entry
Two way traffic
Not fucking here

Now I'm noticing how many graves have flowers!
New flowers!

Signs that the living haunt here.

I'm writing this down, I'm dériving for you
I'm haunting this place
You're here with me
I'm presuming upon your ghosts

(Take plastic flower and lay it on the other objects.)

"You stirred up many feelings
In people in your life, Dad,
But in us only everlasting love"

"Dear Lord why?
Did you take him from me
When you knew I needed him so."

Bernard Stokes
Called to rest on 19th Sept 1973
Brigadier Elsie K. Blunden (retired)
Of the Salvation Army
Blood & Fire

"The following are not permitted:
Glass or plastic vases (or similar), Iron or wooden
Crosses, Enclosed floral tributes, Fencing around graves."

I remember throwing earth on my Gran's coffin; my nephews crying as my Nan's and their Great Nan's coffin slid towards the fire; having stones thrown at me after my old friend Danny's funeral because I was walking through our estate wearing a suit.

The big horse chestnut tree – beneath which I was told Grandad was dead.

It's really dark now, only been here five minutes
I was really excited before
The man comes to lock the gates
Denims and trainers.

I'm going to die,
Nothing noble about it

Attwood Close

A house called Victoriana

Deep Lane

No one smiles here

I'm seeing everything now

I'm seeing great Martian troops striding over the homes

Sunny Take Away

An advertising hoarding covered in lichen – can just make out Captain America

House called Beth Shalom

Facing it a brick hut – a placard says: Albirr Masjid – on the placard there is the illustration of a mosque that looks nothing like this brick hut

A coffee shop, it's 6pm, chairs on the tables

This sure ain't Munich anymore, Toto

Welcome to Basingstoke College of Technology
Access to excellence
5 miles per hour

A teenage girl walks by – other side of the road – on her head a scarf made of the stars and stripes

"Cylinder follows cylinder – the Earth belonged to the martians"

Penrith Road

I found evangelical tracts in the house of the artistic director this morning

Samaritans

And an arrow

That's it.

St Lawrence churches, like this one, are always built on marshland or land recovered from the marshes and no one knows why. Required by an edict of the Roman emperor Valerian (he sounds like a sedative) to produce the treasures of the Christian community, St Lawrence gathered the poor and took them to the emperor. For this he was tortured and killed. Inside the church, the painting of a dragon on a door has eroded, or been scratched away, leaving only its eyes, floating in the wood, like sparks in a canopy of knowing trees.

I pass the point on the beach where Ivan and I had missed the turn for Covehithe yesterday, putting down my rucksack for a moment to apply sun block, I forget my camera; racing back twenty minutes later, passing a puzzled couple I had joked with earlier about the distance to Southwold. "Don't get wet!" they had said. They are from Harwell, Oxfordshire, they say. I say I don't know it and he says "the atomic establishment". The Atomic Energy Research Establishment, "a research laboratory to further the use of nuclear fission for both military purposes and generating energy". The man, otherwise amiable, bridles when I suggest "it was experimental?"

I am on my way to Southwold today and then on to Dunwich tomorrow, the mediaeval city under the water; I am getting closer to the terrain of fire, R'lyeh, a new New York underwater, Cthulhu sleeping between the blocks; did H. P. Lovecraft read up on Dunwich on the subway after borrowing the name? What monster was or is still under there, a few hundred yards offshore? Did they catch it once further south at Orford, the merman, or was it a dragon, all wiped away except for its eyes? "In 1749 The Gentleman's Magazine carried a story concerning several fishermen who were attacked by a winged crocodile-like creature which they snagged in their nets while off this coast. The beast killed one man and disabled another before being slain. The 'sea-dragon' as it came to be known, measured just over a metre in length (though was said to be larger when alive), and possessed two legs with cloven feet. A fisherman travelled the county of Suffolk displaying the creature, though what became of the oddity is unknown."

Racing to retrieve my camera, I can see a second couple back along the beach, but still far off. They have found the camera and are bending over it, opening it up. I do not shout as there are now dogs nearby, but I wave my arms in great windmill motions. After a while the couple see me and wave back. I acknowledge their signal and we meet up. Their dog makes me jump. They feed it a distracting treat. I thank the couple. I start again.

Just before I make Southwold, the 'cliff' above the beach has folded in two steps, and I try to imagine the roar of the land as it ripped, the terror in its unnatural movement.

Coming into Southwold, I walk the gauntlet of witty beach hut names: Redundant Sea, Thelma & Louise, O2B@C, VBlue Jelly 27, Costaplenty, Buckets & Spades, Kippers In A Box, Auntie Bong Bong's, Groyne View. I pass an area of netting securing a road surface; it reminds me of the flattened animals I saw on my second day: Flatland's two-dimensional hedgehogs, rabbits and squirrels. A Punch and Judy booth is in operation.

The wooden rails of the pier are decorated with small celebratory plaques: SUN, SEA, A PINT OF ADNAMS WHAT MORE CAN A MAN WANT AT SIXTY? HAPPY DAYS, BEACH WALKS. A change from the usual memento mori. Is this a historically specific moment, when a prosperous generation retire from work in a way that no future generation will be able to?

The part I like best in a traditional Punch & Judy show is when Jack Ketch, the hangman, in explaining to an 'uncomprehending' Mister Punch how to put one's neck in the noose, in frustration, decides to demonstrate, by placing his own neck there and is strangled by Punch. I like this asymmetrical strategy: persuading the state (by faking stupidity) to use its violence against itself. That is the way to do it. No one on the whole beach is wearing a football shirt. TIM & SARAH GOT WED AND GIGGLED LOTS.

I make my way, determinedly, to the Sailors' Reading Room, expecting something tucked away at the top of a building, but instead find that the Reading Room opens straight onto the promenade and I enter its glassy and polished interior, alone in the clutter and wood panelling, and settle down to read and write. Occasionally, I glance up at the photographs and paintings of fishermen and pilots. They are working men, but not proletarian, they are individualists, cultivating hirsute eccentricities as the marks of their invisible crafts. There is a framed photograph of the Queen Mother in one of the display cases. In the Reading Room, a rare surviving, if museummummified, example of independent, working-class self-education, I get down to work and I write notes for a manifesto:

> The whole industry of heritage is a nightmarish phantasm, running generic narratives with a few eccentric details tacked on the fringes. I suggest reutilising the overspill of excess and the ornaments that overspeak themselves, hollowing out the narratives (which it often does itself until sometimes there really is Nothing There), refusing cultural identity, and building, like good Forteans, from anomalies... a weaving not a fixing – for if you pull them too tight, they will disappear – loose, flexible and in motion, the whole thing never a whole thing, always with

a 'beside' or a 'to one side', always with a view from the wings, looked at as if through a prosthetic extra head (like the decapitated second-heads on martyrs' statues), like St Julian's squint, an interventionist's looking to create situations... The whole of this project is to turn the internal orrery of mythogeography into an external and subversive acting out of mini-situations, passing them on through chatter and journey and social media; an ecology of what we have to gain rather than what we have to lose, a quest, an instability (not a tin can for conservation), a search for meanings. So walking as seeking is crucial to it, it is not desk-bound, nor speeding-by, it is always seeking a way in between, without a set route, not to avoid, but to move between engagement and avoidance, to return for many small encounters, drawing on empirical data from which it sets various practices of information in motion, a kind of 'serious play'... and the concrete crumbling in the field, the power of irrational triggers and mistakes. "By walking between circumstances and the beats of consciousness, the walker can begin to sense the compositional rules of history."

I buy a bottle of Suffolk Apple Juice from the beach café and it is thick with suspended texture. In Gunhill Park a row of cannon and a triangular stone celebrate 'Peace In Europe, 1945'. A Polish threesome chat over it and move on. What peace for their grandparents in 1945?

At the northern end of Gunhill Beach two strange heads are set at the back of one of the beach huts, beneath union jack bunting. They look like parodic mockeries of English soldiers made by Chinese satirists: handlebar moustaches, orientalised features. "Are we standing on a mountain of death?" Are we on a guided tour of the battlefield, just moments after the ceasefire? So forbidding is the figure of the beach hut owner, sentinel at the door, chest puffed, hands locked behind his back, that though I pass up and down the prom three times, I cannot bring myself to speak to him. Do I recognise something in him? A shared criminal tendency that would render me instantaneously transparent to him? Something about him that repels my curiosity by replicating it? The British imperialist process in China, described by Sebald, is unknown; wholly obscured when compared to the general, if limited, consciousness of British involvement in the African slave trade. Yuan Ming Yuan was laid waste simply for being an earthly paradise.

One of the beach huts had been named "Paradise Found". Milton, where is the drama of your un-complacent 'Regained'?

For every good world or welfare state is there an equal obligation on the part of the powerful "to go hunting", to destroy it in the cause of the irrational, in the name of material good? "England meets France!" yells a girl on the beach; she has been digging the Channel Tunnel in sand.

After leaving Ivan and his family, who have joined me for an evening on the beach, I stagger out through Southwold to its suburb on wretchedly blistered feet...

Walking in the Suburbs (2013)

THERE IS SOMETHING UNDERWATER about the sodium lit streets, an occasional drifter on the current, but mostly empty. All the action on small screens indoors. The shadowy alleys are wholly deserted. I am like a citizen patrolman; simply keeping the places peopled. It is almost shocking to walk within a few feet of so many people and to see none of them. Well, one: a small boy in an upstairs room who quickly pulls shut the thick cream-coloured blinds when he sees that I, the new vampire in the neighbourhood, have noticed him. A police patrol car passes; a Ray Bradbury moment. They do not stop. Many people complain that walking the suburbs is mind-destroying. Not if you internalise the details: the zen gravels, the emasculated lawns, the coughs of dogs across the night, and the traces of a long-gone rural terrain. All become metaphorical landscapes across which to plot yourself.

In the daytime, a man throws a bucket of soapy water down his drive, but I see only the water which leaps through the air like an animal. As I pass, I mention this to the man and he cheerfully shouts: "You caught it in the corner of your eye!". Here the voids are tiny ones, but as I explore one the whole tin peels open and I find, sunk beneath the modern surface, a mesh of hollow ways and green lanes hidden behind the house backs, a murder narrative, badgers' sets and kids' dens, a surprise eighteenth-century mansion among bungalows and odd unofficial handwritten posters: one about someone shooting cats, another concerning a mysterious elderly couple sabotaging cars and a third consisting of the desperate pleas of a man from whose care the courts have removed his wife.

...it is always hardest when you get going again after a pause. At ease on the beach, the blisters have swelled and tightened inside my boots.

After settling, cosily, into my B&B, I make my way, grudgingly, back into town, obliged to eat in the Crown Hotel where Sebald ate. I cannot help but eavesdrop on barked conversations. Loud, commanding voices that fit those huge gates, long drives and invisible houses: "lovely girl, she rode with my daughter, and she rode with...."

I wonder about the faces in the last beach hut under Gunhill and reprimand myself.

At the next table: "he hunts at ---------- now." On another table a man is telling stories of terrible falls: from a tree, from a horse, and so on. I eavesdrop on private Last Thursdayisms; relics and genealogies invented right there and then, history customised, a cul-de-sac in the City of God, a missed turn.

The talk turns to the making of social and sexual alliances, the physical rituals of toughness and a certain kind of refined stupidity.

The waves of the 1328 storm at Dunwich 'used' the debris of the first ruined streets as battering rams to destroy the buildings still standing: use the enemy's resources against them, live off their supply lines. Sebald looks out to where Dunwich is buried under the sea. "We beagled round the racecourse." Sebald cites "the immense power of emptiness" ... is that what it is? "Lovely girl..." "very photogenic..." "What?" "She's doing the ------- at Chelsea this year..." Dunwich attracted Swinburne. "O this reminds me, darling, I've just been reading a book about Field Marshall Haig... and in the book it says his father married --------" "O, how fascinating!" "...married into the Bowes-Lyons..." I must look for the last greenish glow on the sea's horizon. Tacita Dean. Donald Crowhurst. I need you now.

The time on the TV display in my bedroom was an hour out. When I ask the waitress she initially tells me the time an hour early and then corrects herself. Time is coming apart here. The aristocracy will last forever. An eternal present foisted on us by Sebald's prose. An artificial hill, green even in midwinter. A guest dashes away to catch the start of *Downton Abbey*, incapable of operating the recorder. The rulers of the universe, combining exact blends of rudeness and good manners: "collapsed in the vicarage".

Sardines, partridge, Binham Blue; the meal is delicious, but over-stimulating, hysterical like Swinburne building vast Lovecraftian fantasy rebellions of peasant-monsters, taxi-driver monsters, rebellions of the organic, of the heatwave, bacteria in the condensation, in the damp heart, monsters in The Mist, rats in the ceiling, fishermen's paper legs in the loft: "we are the bloated men, the going through the motions men, the undigested men, we will live forever men, neither bomb bang or whimper disturbs us, neither is it our past or future, neither its blast nor our conjecture, for we are the bloated men, the upholstered men, the upstanding men, not with a bank, but with a whisper, gone – ....Bowes-Lyons, the Queen Mum, a stowaway in the Sailors Reading Room, the images proliferate, a projected hallucination, scrolls of ideas everywhere. *Uzumaki*. The commercial art gallery here has a "major exhibition of work by Rolf Harris". The clock strikes, the rising of Sebald's sun and moon, and I remind myself to check as I leave. The final tiny chime fades, and so do the stars one by one. The mini-brochure I am handed with the bill, under "Unique Charm", has an image of the fallen tree trunks we passed today; 'dread' too has been commercialised.

After the meal I take a taxi; my feet are shot, I am too tired to worry too much about tomorrow. I say to the driver "make it five pounds" and the driver offers me seven pounds in change. When I pass him my tenner, he hands it back saying that I have already given him the money. I say: "Are you sure?" "O yes." "OK, but why seven pounds?" "O, no... that was my tenner!" he says. And I give him the tenner back, and the two pounds also, and he gives me a receipt for £3.60... The numbers and the hours are melting. Ivan described B&Bs to me as soulless; but they all have different souls; until now at every B&B I have been *asked* what time I want breakfast, but here, Liz, my landlady, *tells* me it is at 8.30am. Time is slipping from my grasp. In the Crown I heard Sebald's clock strike, but forgot to look for it. The missing caryatid in the pub by the ferry. Things are disappearing too. The whole point of this walk, or some point anyway, is slipping away from me.

Multiplicity is the key mythogeographical principle, the principle of multiplicitous narratives and many histories, disrupting the established narratives not only to introduce subaltern ones, but to question the legitimacy of dreamed, felt, feared ones and to invent our own; but where do we go with all this multiplicity? Does it have to pass through a period of loss like this? That the assemblage of multiplicitous narratives, layers, trajectories and so on will almost inevitably lead to some kind of hiatus, a stasis as the mind responds to the multiplicity and its uncapturableness by attempting to reduce it all to some common trait, universal *bon mot,* organic ambience. Does it need a shock to shake the multiple elements back to life? Or a sharp intake of breath and a step back, to make some space for the multiplicitous elements to move themselves? So if I do that about my walk so far what do I see? The palimpsest of churches, hallucinatory and police-like, the marks and portals (and tones) of the ruling folk, the tiny space of the Reading Room. The broad friendliness of the popular founded on the remains of a welfare state (and its self-help hybrid), the mutability of buildings, mutation in general, the ghost of US power in the form of hallucinatory livery and absent airfields, a landscape in which things float, things have gone missing (herring are very slowly returning) like the sailors from the Sailors Reading Room, labour and resistance fixed by a pin to a card in a museum.

The buzz at Southwold Pier, even with its Punch and Judy, felt strong, distinctive, popular (a putting competition was in progress), but in the town, its two bookshops recently closed, its Rolf Harris exhibition, there was a feeling of the Underchalk, of a culture hollowed out from below; and as I had walked up the shingle between a broad and the sea, and said to myself "where's the danger?" my leg sank down a yard, like a bus into a Norwich road, and after that I felt that the whole surface might be unsupported. All day walking, I had thought it was the 1st not the 2nd of October. The days are slipping, the currency, the contracts, I am beginning to worry about making wrong assumptions, nothing on the TV is watchable, I hear the clock ticking like a bass drum. All day, it had only been in the Sailors Reading Room that I had any focus or steadiness at all. Perhaps I should seek out similar sites, havens of independent thought, anachronisms that trip up the mummery of 'time stood still'... I need to sleep, to find some healing stasis there.

3.10.11

For the first time, clouds. Up till now it has been "Crab Man weather": the phrase my publisher uses to describe the incidence of good weather that seems to hang upon my walking. Over the course of a hundred performances and drifts and days on long walks, I have only ever walked in rain three or four times, and have mostly walked in brilliant sunshine, a meteorological strike rate that, given that most of my walking has been in England, wavers between good fortune and disturbingly charmed (I will have ruined it now, though, writing this).

On the horizon (from my bedroom) no watchtower churches, but a huge water tower on concrete stilts and what looks like a silo for the docks. Last night I was thrown; the "good pub grub" sign outside had not prepared me for those upper class tones. I heard the clock strike thinly, both for eight and nine, yet did not see its mechanism; I do not feel it left me well.

At breakfast, Joan, a fellow guest here at '49', puts my blisters in perspective; she walked 26 miles yesterday; some of the keener of her fellow marathon walkers are going at four and a bit miles per hour. What can they see, what do they engage with?

Soon after setting off, I meet and chat with an elderly man on the path to the old railway bridge over the Blyth. He has a barking dog called Herbie. The man tells me that Herbie once found 72 golf balls on a single walk, and that he has 800 golf balls at home, that he is blind in one (1) eye so I am to walk on his good side. He tells me how he and his wife once had a business making gentlemen's neckties, supplying smart West End shops, and that he once made sixteen (16) ties for the Prince of Wales. It starts to rain. The man tells me that he and his wife eventually set up their own retail company, but that he has been retired 31 years now. I begin to wonder whether this old fellow is one of the ascended masters, favouring me with a numerological code: 72, 800, 1, 16, 31. He tells me that during the war he was stationed nearby, and then, after D-Day he joined the advance on Berlin. On April Fools' Day in 1945 (one four one nine four five) he was on the outskirts of the German capital, in an armoured car, when a sniper, out of nowhere, fired and hit the tank. The bullet went into his arm, a chip of paint dislodged from the tank blinded him in the right eye: the eye that floats, to add to the decapitated or open head. The paint was not metallic so the surgeons were unable to remove it. Two days later the same armoured car – with this man now far away in hospital – was hit by artillery fire and all his comrades killed.

After the war, he was involved in experimental work nearby, "trying to make tanks fly". He laughs and describes chaotic experiments in ditches and rockets tied to unmanned tanks. Now he plays golf three times a week. I tell him that I play bowls and he tells me that he did also, even rose so high as to captain "so called", he says, the Sole Bay Bowling Club, whose green I had passed earlier, but that he had got into a dispute on the rink with another player over the lie of a wood. He shows me with the forefinger and thumb of a blotchy hand the distance under dispute; a quarter of an inch, (now we are into fractions!) "Well, if you want it that bad", he had said "you can have it, mate" and he never played again. "I've still got my woods – in fact I'm wearing my bowling shoes now." He shows me the flat soles of his shoes.

In the mis-guided tours that I perform, the multiplicities of factoids and the linearity of the route are both equally decried and travestied as they are performed; exorcised on the spot, so they can then return in transparent forms as pseudo-ritual acts (simple in themselves, but made potent by the double-movement of exorcism and spectral return). So, what is the double-movement manoeuvre that comes between the solo or single tactics that I use on a journey like this one and its raising to a next level of counter-walking? What will sustain this transfiguration beyond a simple accumulation (of, say, 800 golf balls)? Maybe it will be ordeal; the giant blisters that seem to fill my boots and squeeze my toes out from their usual positions? I had had to brave Herbie's barking and showing his long white teeth in order to speak to the blotched crypto-numerologist; and I was rewarded with stories and numbers.

At the private landing 'stages' on the Blyth river, the slip with the local taxi firm's number, kept in case my feet finally give up, escapes and I chase it down the wooden walkway like the characters chasing the runes in *The Night of the Demon* (M.R. James, again); where was that story set? Around here?

Until yesterday afternoon, when I started looking for Ivan and his family, I was very happy and comfortable in my disruption, but their domestic presence has disrupted my disruption! I have exacerbated this by my lack of inscrutability at '49', putting myself unintentionally into the domain of the 'ideal'. Now I can only move to a new level: through ordeal or crisis, to a new multiplicity. It certainly is an ordeal to get to Dunwich; hardly very far, but walking in the shingle is like wading in a treacle full of hammers. Avoiding dogs. Watching sand martins, huge dragonflies in the livery of thousand bomber raids, egret ghosts. The stretched vistas do strange things: a couple up ahead turn into a notice board...

"Not everything that walks is a psychogeographer."

...another couple with a black and white dog turn into a couple with a white dog; a fallen tree trunk metamorphoses into the couple from Harwell and their spaniel which growls at me when I walk off playing the follower in *Whistle And I'll Come To You*, the thing on the beach. Distance transforms things, time winds things tight, rolls them up. I walk for twenty minutes and Dunwich gets no closer...

Doppel

You MIGHT HAVE NOTICED that the couple from Harwell appear on two beaches on consecutive days. Although I only remember meeting them once, my notebook records both meetings on both beaches. I had somehow known from the start that something like this would happen: "I will be walking *towards* immobility... painfully aware that what I am doing is a copy of a copy..."

..."We were in a nature reserve and this... it was like a Star Trek thing... and it didn't twig for a couple of minutes..." I grasp upon this shard of overheard conversation outside the café at the edge of Dunwich. Please don't let this be the *only* café in Dunwich; there is something vaguely detergent-like in my Earl Grey. The huge portions of fish and chips all around me are strangely intimidating. Ah, the couple from Harwell are in the café; somehow I knew I would see them, perhaps they are drawn by the energy here? Like me, edging their way along the coast to Sizewell? A couple of fishermen are preparing their nets on Dunwich beach.

Rejecting the food at the café, I find the pub. I know those voices... it's them again! The people from the Crown Hotel in Southwold last night have turned up today as part of a walking party at The Ship in Dunwich. I remember that they had referred to a walk last night and here they are, under the shaded veranda, around a huge table, all in white and the palest of blues, luminescent in the unseasonable sunlight, describing their struggles with new technology: "a round tower talk... things do date terribly... the squire... ha ha ha... we had a phone call from (student daughter) to say that we didn't pack the egg cups!"

Did Dunwich really rival London as an early mediaeval port or has its importance increased each time its sorry tale has been told? I would not begrudge it the exaggeration, at all. This is a mythogeographical hub – like Cockington, A la Ronde, Morte Point, Bory Var, the gardens of the Walnut Museum in the Dordogne – a place that provide models, ordeals and mysteries as means to experience and explore other sites.

Mediaeval Dunwich conducted its trade "without the protection of any powerful nobleman" (I am reading pamphlets bought from the museum next door), mounting their own defence; its destruction by the sea was retribution, as in Machen's *The Terror*, for their defiance of hierarchy. Dunwich's traders, when faced with the offers and demands of rebellion in 1173, chose to be loyal to the King; threatened with extermination by the rebels, everyone fought: "not a wife or a girl, who did not to the palisade carry a missile". Swinburne's writing about Dunwich is stunning; but is he duplicitous? His initial sublime terror is thunderous, but as he seeks redemption he is both ambiguous and subservient. There is no "HERE" in Dunwich for "YOU" to "ARE".

I follow the Dunwich Guide 'Trail', the map purchased from the Museum, passing a community noticeboard on which is pinned a cartoon of a City broker stealing money from accounts (o, maybe I was wrong), an MP fiddling expenses and a rioter in a hoodie looting Adidas trainers. Written in longhand over the cartoon is "coincidence?". With the Cuban Missile Crisis Baby, at the Lowestoft B&B, I had discussed how people had turned against the looters. He thought the looters were surprised at the animosity. I wondered if what isolated them was not the looting itself, but the manner of it, the attacks on small shops and people's homes above them, and, above all, the robbery from an injured Malaysian student: the battle of images was lost.

Did a spirit of independence and dissidence persist here? It strikes me how close Orford is to 'Little Moscow'.

The Dunwich Guide 'Trail' takes me to the Leper Chapel at St James's Church; a lepers' hospital was still operating here into the 1800s. The illness came back from the Middle East with the crusaders; a passenger of an earlier globalisation. A buttress of All Saints' Church, rescued from the very edge of the cliff top, now stands in St James's churchyard, a monumental wormhole to precariousness. I pass a group of schoolchildren being led through the ruins of Greyfriars Priory. "DO NOT CLIMB ON THE RUINS" – yes, do, climb on the ruins!

In the woods near the remnants of Greyfriars Priory I find an insect sculpture, exactly as I make them, put together from fallen boughs.

On my way back to the heart of the village, I pass along Long Row, built to house those 'freemen' of Dunwich evicted from their homes for refusing to vote for their sitting MP in a 'rotten borough' election: George Downing, the property speculator responsible for building Downing Street. Effigies were burned, 'freemen' were threatened, spies operated in the village. A new MP thought that further threats of evictions were justified to prevent those small beginnings from which revolutions grow. A later squire, St John Barne, was responsible for protecting Queen Victoria from Fenian terrorists. Since Somerleyton, I wonder if I am walking here in the suburb of the British State.

Downing built a confabulated classical/gothic facade around the Greyfriars Priory ruins, enclosing his private residence, a jail, the ruins and a town hall; an early privatisation. Later, a Blue Room and a Green Room were added. "And Dunwich dreams", wrote Ernest Read Cooper. Sleeping with Cthulhu, presumably. Glug glug. In the late nineteenth century, writers and artists flocked here; attracted by the human remains from the churchyard of All Saints tumbling down the cliff face. Bits of All Saints ended up in a rockery at the Chelsea Flower Show; subject of a conversation at the Crown Hotel last night. Is there still a Bishop of Dunwich, created 1934? Yep. In J.M.W. Turner's painting, All Saints' Church emits an unearthly, silvery glow; walking the miles of shingle to Dunwich today, all the time there had been just such a field of sunlight on the sea ahead, where the sunken city is burning, yearning beneath, phosphorescent, its bells rung by the obscene and distended organs of the great Cthulhu. It is sometimes said that the 'little freemen of Dunwich' rowed out to sea over the old 'city' to vote; depends what you mean by 'vote', I suppose; votives as much as voters, perhaps? No wonder the portraits in the Reading Room were of such unclassifiables. I am walking north of the village now, where black phantom dogs, Suffolk Shock, eyes "as big as saucers" are sometimes sighted: Herbie, perhaps. I had shown him just enough respect and he had protected me on the path all day.

When the whole of Dunwich was put up for sale in 1947, the estate agents were Jackson Stops; a wormhole to my Hurst Walk, during which I passed The Jackson Stops pub in Stretton, Rutland, so re-named because the estate agents' 'For Sale' sign had hung over it for so long.

Back at the Museum I ask the curator about Sebald's statement that "until about 1890 what was known as Eccles Church Tower still stood on Dunwich beach" and she points out that the actual and obvious place for Eccles Church Tower is Eccles, about 50 miles to the north. We discuss whether Sebald purposefully blurs things, is as lackadaisical as Motion, or whether the point is that the distinction is insignificant. Historical ruins were once regarded as primarily aesthetic objects, she says; manipulations at Stonehenge and Avebury were attempts to bring the stones closer to a neo-classicist ideal. Sebald was reshuffling the coastline of Melancholia, not an empirical or geological one.

Dunwich Museum was originally sited at the Rocket Station. Things move around. This visit has rekindled my feeling for the museum-surreal: an information video featuring Saxons in spotlessly clean shirts, a mannequin startled by visitors, an endless array of variations on the same artefact over which the eye glazes and passes on, stuffed things. Why not just exhibit the frames and the stuffing, the before and after and forget the rest? This is why Dunwich is so mythogeographically strong: its story keeps going missing. The photographic sequence of the gradual collapse of All Saints, the lines on the 3D map showing the different stages of the mediaeval town's inundation, the piece of All Saints at St James's, the museum's own history of itself, and its curator: these are its treasures.

The curator, who is very open to the idea of allowing ruins to decay and disappear, tells me of a TV programme connecting the locations of dragon myths to finds of large dinosaur fossils. I wonder how that fits the dragon that Sebald describes on the old Southwold–Halesworth steam train.

I swear that one of the locals drinking in The Ship right now appears as a Saxon in the Museum's video. Flies land on me continually; as if I were already a corpse. Eavesdropping on bar conversations, I pretend to read about the 1802 'Battle of Dunwich': at 2am villagers were woken by flashing lights and explosions. The Terror. 'Something like a cannonball' hit a stable wall, then Silence. A large form was seen sailing away, a smaller one approaching. On the 'cannonball' was a BROAD ARROW (the mark of the British State) but the Admiralty denied any involvement. The incident remains a mystery. I drink pints of Molly's Secret, Adnam's Southwold and Broadside and then head for my B&B at Little Greyfriars; it is about 300 yards from the top of its curling drive to the front door. On my way out again, using a borrowed torch from the landlady, going for dinner at The Ship, I am mistaken for a burglar. I am checking whether I have read the OS map correctly, waving the torch beam across the hedgerows to identify the mouth of the Suffolk coastal path for the morning. The light disturbs a neighbour who comes out to challenge me. The roads are quiet now, but there are eyes on me again. I explain myself as best I can, turn and make an intriguing half-mile walk to The Ship along the dark lane. As I pass the priory ruins the temperature drops abruptly and then rises just as suddenly. A soft, warm glow ebbs from a nearby house; just the feel I once got from homes I would pass in my childhood, homes I longed to call at, spontaneously, without reason, to see if a whole new life might just begin that way.

Some talk of rockets at the bar. A man: "I want a trike, so I'm going to get it, if you want something then go for it, that's a healthy approach to life... though, of course, I need to think about it first." Lucy Maud Montgomery, author of *Anne of Green Gables*, wrote that Dunwich folk were "the most hopelessly stupid folk I have ever tried to extract information from". Maybe they were intelligently evasive? "I'm a rummy man, I'm not a poker man", says the trike man. "It feels like everything's changing", the barman says.

I read in the local paper that one of the empty bookshops in Southwold closed due to the suicide of its owner.

The local Freemen's Oath, "the secrets and consells of the town you shall not betray", local author Ormonde Pickard contends, is the origin of the Official Secrets Act. Up until the sale in 1947, the village was an estate village, but after that it became dominated by holiday makers and retirees. Liz, this morning, was very down on what has happened to Southwold, saying that local people prefer Reydon, its suburb, now. Only in the winter do the locals get their town back.

A few highlights from other drifts and wanders (2)

⁷Ḥ With my very young daughter trespassing through Budapest vestries in search of the severed hand of Saint Istvan.

⁷Ḥ Being mistaken for the ghost of a monk in the Valley of the Rocks.

⁷Ḥ A porter at the George Hotel at Stamford peeling back a carpet in the cocktail lounge, opening a trapdoor and leading me down into the hidden remains of an eleventh-century chapel of Mary Magdalene.

⁷Ḥ Making a walk with Jason's help through a residential area that had once been the grounds of Scott of the Antarctic's childhood home, we were approaching an account of Scott's death, turned the corner, and in front of a block of flats, children had erected a play tent...

⁷Ḥ Out of my head, early Saturday night, pink sports paper in hand, wandering into the downstairs bar of Yates Wine Lodge, Nottingham, and stepping directly into the late 1940s.

⁷Ḥ With a drifting group, passing a group of ramblers on a narrow path; and as if both groups knew they were walking in different dimensions, neither the dérivistes nor the ramblers said a single word nor exchanged a single glance.

⁷Ḥ Calling on a care home during a week-long walking quest with Uncle Tacko and Aeolian Hugh, I met an old man who showed me a picture he had painted of Stonehenge by, he said, living out the experiences of each of its stones.

⁷Ḥ Dancing with Siriol on the coppery heights of Mynydd Parys.

ʰḤ Being smuggled with Bess into the Templar Church near the Strand
by a kind usher.

ʰḤ Finding 'Q' and 'R' on cobbles under the gravel of Horse Guards
Parade.

4.10.11

This morning I am due to walk past the Sizewell B nuclear reactor, crossing Dunwich
Heath, scene of Machen's 'Terror'. Sebald became lost here, panicking, as in the
Somerleyton Hall maze. "Please speak no more, I am walking with ghosts – by
Dunwich shore." (J. W. Gosling).

Above the breakfast things at Little Greyfriars, across shelf after shelf, are
lined in smart attention the theosophical works of the likes of Madame Blavatsky
and Alice A. Bailey. I am particularly taken by the copy of *The Soul* by D. K., the
initials standing for Djwal Khul, who, of course, coordinates the seven masters of
the Seven Rays, the seventh of which is the Count of Saint Germain whose Ray is,
according to Bailey, expressed in radioactivity...

Cryptic

THE WORLD IS FULL of very strange things and most of them, most of the time, stare us straight in the face and we do not see them. These may include the esoteric arrows under benchmarks or the sacred symbols smuggled into corporate logos and onto manhole covers. They may have something to do with origins: any building made of limestone mostly comprises billions of tiny brachiopod corpses; people are mostly made up of dead stars. Some things just have weird names; one size of traffic cone is named after the Bigfoot cryptid. To spot these things you need some curiosity, a conscious inhibition of your brain's natural editing process and a willingness to spend time immersed on the fringes of science and symbology.

...leather bound, these volumes are not a casual collection, but first editions, deeply thumbed, the library of a mystically-inclined supernaturalist practising a century ago. For some reason I am unable to speak of the books to the landlady. What do I recognise in her, what she in me?

Little Greyfriars is one of three houses constructed out of a single giant Greyfriars, built for the anti-Fenian Banes; three in one.

On Dunwich Heath my panic is present, but entirely limited and under control, mastered, aesthetic and deeply enjoyable. Alone on the Heath, among the bleakness of a mass of gorse and fern, a jay flashes me a green signal and I "GO". A way off, towards the power station, bright warning lights are blinking. Machines move about.

I love the dread of the Heath and I move with it, pretending I am Malcolm McDowell's Mick Travis in *O Lucky Man!* with the moor all about me alight from the explosion at the nuclear facility and me in the gold lamé suit; then I drink from a stream among the flames and radioactive mists and walk on, across the *to apeiron* of Anaximander's unenclosed infinity, part wasteland and part birthplace, looking for the church that will suckle me; the church where Mick is born again into a walker, a bear of a man with a rugged staff, striding across the fields towards the motorway. In parallel to him, I walk along a long peopleless beach to Sizewell B. "It's the Moon Project!" I can be in *Quatermass II*, or *Alternative Three*, as well as *O Lucky Man!* Three in one. I measure out my life with Gaumont tickets. The great dome of the B plant looms and lures. What alien is growing inside... me? There is no you for here to be.

I find a massive piece of landing stage, a chunk of quayside ripped and tossed onto the beach. How stable is this shore? Cthulhu B. A reactor under the sea.

A white "camera equipped" police van drives out to have a look at me. Then another.

On Sizewell beach is a memorial, a snapped paddle cast in bronze, to the 32 young Dutch men who attempted to escape here in kayaks from Nazi-occupied Holland; eight made it, three survived the war.

A third police van passes me on the road into Leiston, overtakes and immediately swings around and turns back towards the plant; they're not just watching me, but letting me know they are watching me. As John, the local who later helps me, will say: "this is the problem in a small town, knowing everyone." I am comfortable being a stranger. Outside the gates of Sizewell B is The Vulcan Arms with a pub sign depicting the god Vulcan, Mister Spock (a Vulcan) and a V (Vulcan) bomber. Do the authorities at the plant welcome the association of civil nuclear power with nuclear weapons? I feel absurdly nervous as I walk towards Leiston; another police van passes me by. Maybe it is the same one again and again. Walking beneath the power cables I feel the huge dark cold force of the rush of souls. Another police van overtakes me, just as I abruptly turn into an old siding to examine some derelict stock; when I re-emerge I find the nuclear cops in a tizzy over my apparent vanishing into thin air. I give them a nod, which they ignore and race off.

In Leiston I am wary of the workers in the café; gazed upon with sustained suspicion, I have begun to feel shady. "How safe is nuclear, remember Japan in the war" says a graffito.

After a salad, I set off down Aldeburgh Road to look for my grandfather at an address I have found on a strip of paper in the little case that holds his sharpshooter medal, awarded in 1927. Walking on the hard roads today, I remember why I like them so much. On such even surfaces I can keep my gaze up all the time. But the numbers of the houses run out long before the 83 on the slip. I ask a man who is working on his house, John, and he sends me to see a Mister Wright back at a house called Holly Wood. Is something messing with me here? "He's got cancer in the face so he looks a bit, you know, but he's fine", says John. Mister Wright's face is a purple river system. He is as sharp as a pike's tooth. "I was here in 1927!" he says with joy. But he can't remember the houses ever having numbers. He asks for Grandad's name and when I say "Harry Smith" he says "it rings a bell" – a bell in Dunwich-Under-The Sea – but he can't put a face to the name. Having thanked Mister Wright for his trouble, I return to John the DIY man, who offers to drive me further down the road. We set off; me suddenly mindful that both W.G. Sebald and Charles Hurst (the two men whose journeys I have recreated) died in cars.

John drives in an *exploratory* manner. We track back to the early even numbers, then swing around and head for Aldeburgh, stopping to speak to a thin woman, and then at the local laundry where a woman remembers a "Vincent-Smith" two doors down. When John tells me that some of the houses on Aldeburgh Road were "Garnett houses" – homes for Garnett factory workers or servants at the Garnetts' big house – I wonder if Gran, a servant, might have worked for the Garnetts. Was that what brought Grandad here? Dad was born in

1930 so the timing would make sense. We ambush the postwoman, but she tells us there are no numbers, only house names.

John drops me at the museum in town, where they are equally stumped by the issue of house numbers on Aldeburgh Road. The woman on the counter rings her postman husband; but there is no breakthrough. I enjoyed the absurd adventure with John; what were we looking for exactly? Sometimes it is just as good to *not* find things; it puts you to one side of your own efforts, drawing an outline of what is missing, of what it is no longer possible to regain.

I buy a couple of pamphlets from the museum shop, then notice on the display stand the familiar blue cover of a handbook on the maintenance of stationary steam engines, written by one 'C. Hurst' – it's the Charles Hurst of my 2009 walk! The two walks have crossed. Things are weaving for me now, I have thrown myself at this landscape and its tendrils have borne me up on a litter of charred sward.

Leiston's reputation as 'Little Moscow' has its origins, appropriately, in the ruination of the major manufacturers here, Garnett's, when the owners' rock solid investment in Tsarist Government bonds was rendered worthless by the Bolshevik revolution. The business never quite recovered and the Garnett family eventually sold off its large residence on the edge of the town. Referred to by John as "The School", the Garnetts' house became 'Summerhill', A.S.Neill's progressive school. Some of the first teachers there were Communist Party members or supporters and had a powerful impact on the town through political education, the regular publication of a radical local paper, *Leiston Leader,* and activism, notably organising for the Norwich to London hunger march to come through the town in 1934. This was the time of the famous Jarrow Hunger March which brought my Uncle Billy Buxton to Coventry; he and my Great Uncle Bill debated communism versus capitalism in front of our assembled family. When I asked which side prevailed, my Nan said "O, Billy Buxton, he was a great talker!", but the result did not seem to have changed anybody's mind much.

Richard Webster, author of the pamphlet 'Suffolk's Little Moscow', describes Leiston as "a fascinating museum of the history of the last two centuries"; to be added to the pantheon of mythogeographical hubs, all the more potent for a spectre of Communism double-spectred and Sizewell A cooling until 2027.

The communists in Leiston made coalitions with religious non-conformists, and with the Labour Left. I helped to build the equivalent of such coalitions in the 1980s in Bristol, until I was persuaded by rational argument to abandon that approach for a narrower one, refusing any longer to give 'left cover for reformism'. It was a terrible mistake; politically and humanly. And when I think of the death of my closest comrade of those coalition years, my friend WB, and I think of him often, and when I think of the things that he did after I had lost any real touch with him and did not renew proper contact when I knew I should, I see, from the things I learned at his funeral, how each of us was in those years apart moving quickly towards what the other was doing. I have no illusions about anything I might have done that would have changed how things ended, but I should have been there to try. And would have been if I had stuck to my instinctive politics; a comradeship of differences and negotiations. I failed at all the levels.

My friend WB's genius was to see the constructedness of things; the trajectories of materials, to trace the tendrils of production; he had a soft spot for 'Stalinists', but was scrupulously democratic in his own behaviour towards others. Thanks to my stupidity and stasis I will not have the opportunity to argue with him again. In *The Rings Of Saturn* today I re-read Sebald's writing on the death of William Browne. I walk through countryside-as-desert. I sense everywhere the erosion from the landscape of the extraordinary pasts of ordinary people. The eternal present of total obliteration. Never to argue with WB again. Nevernevernevernevernever. Melancholia going on forever; a latent landscape of private horrors, unreliable surfaces and missing things. There is no *reason* in it.

Chatting to Dad on my mobile as I sit in a bus shelter in Snape, he says that Grandad's crackshot ability meant that he was in demand for shooting parties when on leave, coaching the aristocratic shots, but not above standing behind the shooters and picking off birds for the shooters to claim as their own kills; that might also explain why he was in the proximity of a large house like that of the Garnetts. Our connections to The Powers: Gran as servant, Grandad as armed coach and fabulist. I am beginning to wonder at Grandad's silence. If he survived four years in the trenches, a good enough shot to time his trigger pull to that of unskilled aristocrats, discreetly taking down their birds for them, how many men, far bigger targets than grouse, might he have killed in four years. Had the numbers numbed, or did there come a dialectical moment for Grandad when a quantitative addition became a qualitative change and the arithmetic added up into human beings; meat and blood on the ground.

I check into my Snape B&B, then wander down the hill to a gastro-pub for dinner, where I am an involuntary eavesdropper: "her rudeness was part of her charm, once you got to know her. He was very worried about her, you know, very worried when he was dying, he said 'you won't stop coming to see her will you?'" A young bloke comes in, who, when asked by the barmaid how he is, says: "terrible since you left here the other night" and then he stands, moonstruck, for a good half an hour; he seems to be hoping that *something*, her, fate, destiny, will help him out here; then he leaves, abruptly, performing the hurt and humiliation he surely feels for real and raw. This is like watching myself in a timeslip with Laura Zunz, standing over the manhole I had fallen into the night before. "I love you." "Do you feel better having said that?" Gawd help us. Touch of genius in that choice of location. I got a play out of it, though: *A Bottle of Hirondelle*. That way I got to fall in love with entire audiences. Weirdly, Laura, you came to see it (how did you hear about it? did you know?). That was the only time I saw you after the manhole declaration. It is 36 years too late, I know, but I do still think of watching you backstage, falling in love with you as you stitch my costume, and, just to say, I lied: the correct answer was "no". It still is "no". Pathetic, really. The barmaid is remarkable for her confident, uncompromising lack of response. She is admirable. Meanwhile, I am becoming properly paranoid; I think I am overhearing a plot at the bar to attack Derek Jarman's home at Dungeness.

I go back to the B&B and watch Ken Russell's *Elgar* on the dvd player in my bedroom; some of the shots seem to have been filmed in the field behind Mum and Dad's bungalow, with the Malvern Hills in the background, the field where I would walk when I needed a moment alone so as to return more fully to Mum's dying, Mum's last living, a life in hours and minutes. Once you have a multiplicity in motion, coincidence becomes the norm...

Coincidences

ON A DRIFT OF EXETER WITH KOREAN and Saudi language students, we repeatedly encountered a blue stencil graffito of a young woman's face on the walls of offices and shops around the High Street. I speculated that the image was that of a 40s' movie star. We stopped at an example of her blue face on the white stone of a Co-op supermarket when she – the model for the stencil graffiti – suddenly appeared, and saw, to her delight and our surprise, her blue and white image for the very first time.

I took a group of students on a walk along a spit of dunes, setting them various tasks: to write a poem over the next hundred metres and to recite it, to lift together the heaviest thing in view, and so on. On the beach we found a much eroded and staggered wooden groyne; looking more like an art work than a sea defence, it made a strong impression on the group. Later, I asked the students to go on 'quests'; one set for herself the target of walking to distant hills she had often looked out to, but never visited. Without a map she felt her way across the landscape towards the hills, running out of roads and public footpaths she walked tentatively up a farm track on which she met the landowner, who directed her past his barn, inviting her to look in if she wished, and beyond that to the fields she sought. In the barn she found a small studio and in that a painting of the staggered wooden groyne.

'sploring

One of the great things about not knowing where you are going is that relatively unimpressive landscapes, structures or artefacts take on a new aura and wonder when stumbled across or encountered as part of a walking narrative. What, if planned, might be found with some minor self-satisfaction, can instead be encountered as a staggering discovery, a bone-stopping association, a punch in the heart accusation from the past, a precious mis-design; some rotted shed, some parts of a shattered wing mirror like self-fracturing selves, some stream in a suburban valley, a sodium lamplit beauty... these unfold one after the other, space unravelling rather than delivering.

...and you sense just how connected the world really is; the terrain about you, metaphorical and material, becomes a supportive sward, holding you up as if you

116

are walking on top of the corn stalks. Separation is rare in nature. My separateness from WB was never some 'natural' drifting apart as I liked to tell myself, nor a falling out as others had imagined, but my chosen, contrary, cowardly refusal of the co-incidence that our two lives, even then, still bent towards. I will never argue with him again. Neverneverneverneverever.

...you might feel it is time to take a walk, to have a break from words for awhile. And if some provocation would help:

Walk as bones
Walk as if alone
Walk flowingly as blood
Walk stuck
Walk as shit
Walk walk's walk
Walk as walk walks
As two streams of sweat
As work
As sex
Walk with the path
With the hills
With the final groves
With sadness
With tending, attention, attending, tenderness

Walk like a wound

Walk like the Fall
Walk like the Deluge
Walk when your footprints run out
Walk like Revelation
Walk till the end
And then
Again

Take both roads
Where they split in the woods
Like sex
Walk out of the pages
Just before
The book snaps shut

Walk drawing

Walk like a besom
Walk like chalk
Walk like an errand gone errant

Carry a table
Or the heaviest thing you are able to
Carry a miniature theatre in your pocket
Walk sensitive to the stories that are snagging at your ankles
Fixate on symbols you don't understand

Carry a torch in the daytime
Carry a mask in the dark

5.10.11

White deer. Nuns and stained glass. My landlady tells me to look out for a white deer as I walk along the edge of Rendelsham Forest today. As she talks, I think of the baby white Sperm Whale I saw on a TV documentary and how I wondered if, me at 90 and it mature, I could swim into its jaws, I think of polar bears stuffed and drowning and hermaphrodite, I dimly recall seeing a white deer many years ago on the Quantock Hills, just after reading *The White Goddess* by Robert Graves; the incarnation of his reference to a white hind caught in a thicket. I had seen it among a herd of deer, tangled in a cluster of antlers...

Note

ALTHOUGH I WAS ONLY DIMLY AWARE of its significance, a vein of colour symbolism had begun to run through my walk: firstly, the white of the deer I first heard about in Snape, and subsequently symbols of black, red and finally gold.

Given the region of fire that my walk was soon to pass through, an area something akin to a crucible, it is hard to not to see the parallels with a jumbled alchemy: the purification in the white albedo, the decomposition of the black nigredo, the burning in the yellow light and solar fire of citrinitras, and the end of it all in red rubedo.

...the kitchen of Albion House (it is hard not to come over all symbolical here) is decorated with angels and sanderlings, and an improving text: "The difference between Heaven and Hell is in the thinking". Not for everyone.

On the radio: news of spreading Occupy Wall Street actions. A conservative US commentator is assuring us that unlike the demonstrations in Greece or Tahrir Square, these are "just theatrics", citing the involvement of the labour unions.

I suppose it must look like that if you think the world consists of performances for hire. My landlady tells me that Albion House was once a tiny convent and that baptisms and other ceremonies were held in the lounge. The stained glass window, with its Latin motto, was taken away to be restored; but the glazier was no classics scholar and jumbled the words when he put it back. I enjoy the accidental poetry, but I leave the house, mildly discomforted by its mildness.

Once outside I am filled with the joy I feel everyday on setting out from the door of a B&B or the lobby of a hotel; delighted by a prospect of certain pleasure of some kind and unknown territory for falling in love with, uncertain if anybody will ever have felt it quite like I will. Each day, turning myself into a fool who knows nothing, I have a chance to learn everything again, to make something new from the base materials of everyday places...

> "Everybody knows about Tintern; but it is given to few to
> be learned in the science of the lanes between Llandegfeth
> and Llangibby, or to have viewed the carved rood-screen of
> Partrishow on the mountain side."
>
> Arthur Machen

...this is the alchemy of walking: not to seek pleasures but to invent new ones...

The wobbly art of memory

'THE ART OF MEMORY' is a mental technique that allows a person to memorise and recall extremely complex and detailed esoteric information by ascribing different concepts and passages to the specific features of an imagined landscape. When mentally returning to that memorised landscape the concepts or texts can be visualised and recalled by walking through the features to each of which has been allotted an idea. But in my 'wobbly art of memory' the complex ideas and texts are ascribed to real landscapes that are subject to erosion, demolition, and so on – so that as the material world changes it jumbles, fragments, edits and overturns the philosophy.

...I pass through Tunstall Forest looking unsuccessfully for a white deer. Emerging from the trees onto the Common I look instead for UFOs and there is one, landed in a distant field, a huge white dome on the horizon, and I wonder if I am looking back to Sizewell and yesterday. As I had passed the cooling core of A reactor there had come a sound from it like that of the flying saucers in *UFO*, Gerry Anderson's mixed animation/live-action TV show.

UFOs were a great cover story for the blotchy man's post-war experiments with rocket-powered tanks, I think. Just outside the perimeter fence of the former Bentwaters Air Base stands the church of St John the Baptist; sheep sit at the door, a fiercely distorted gargoyle face glowers on a lintel. Were the bombs blessed? I am not surprised to see a large mansion house close by. I have noticed before the proximity of large estates to military facilities; ancient buffers.

In Rendelsham Forest, I walk among ruined concrete installations, bases of small buildings and openings for bunkers. I find a couple of larger features: a tunnel and something vague by the roadside in pieces...

Holey space

THE 'NDRANGHETA, a mafia organisation in Sicily, has created underground networks of tunnels in which dead ends, false tunnels, hidden trapdoors and other distractions are built in to keep the uninitiated out.

...jewels of the military Underchalk. Subterranean concrete monsters, their shadows thrown up into landscape. The sand underfoot is always shifting. I meet no one else walking. The commercial units at Bentwaters come straight out of *Quatermass II*; wherever you are in the Suffolk landscape, Winnerton Flats is never far away: concrete roads and perimeter fences. Water sprays across giant fields from large serpentine machines. I am towered over by three huge *Quercus robur*, black against a momentarily universally blue sky, acorns fall, pinging me hard on the head and leaves shake with a roar like an alien ventilation system. So many connections: oaks, Hurst's manual, the field behind Mum and Dad's. Love you, Mum. I walk across a carpet of crab apples; the final straw for the Dowager Empress Tz'u-hsi, who succumbed to a double helping with clotted cream. A yellow Rolls Royce glistens on a camping site. Lady Penelope's pink Rolls was parked in a drive visible from my grammar school classroom. A scarlet RAF fire engine passes by. A metallic caterpillar crawls along the road. Yesterday there were purple fields around Sizewell, and purple rivers crossing Mister Wright's cheeks. Today, there is purple heather on Tunstall Common.

I see a chalked advert for a band called *The Trembling Wheelbarrows* and a house called 'Arcadia': 'et in East Anglia ego'. Paintbox poppies by the roadside. And a witty concrete horseshoe kerb at the mouth of a bridleway. A field covered in plastic that at first I think is a field of waves. Then, after a pint of Wherry bitter at The British Larder (Michelin star, cannot afford to eat there, sadly) on to the mildly terrifying main road into Woodbridge. No pavement and 70mph lorries.

In Woodbridge I ask at a number of bookshops, charity stores and the TIC for anything on the Rendelsham Forest UFO flap; no one has anything. They look at me as if I have requested some particularly ripe variety of porn.

In Caffè Nero, Woodbridge's equivalent of Dunwich's 'go for it' man is in action: loudly punching above his weight. He is witty, jolly and charming, grinning like a blowtorch through his errors, his inner seriousness disconnected very slightly, so some part of his rhetorical project is always flapping about like an unhinged plank.

In Church Street, in the window of a vacated antiques shop is a dilapidated model of Woodbridge's main square; abjection in miniature.

A pair of compasses on a building signifies a freemasonic owner.

I see for a second time an eccentric looking man carrying huge, overflowing plastic bags; he has long black and grey hair and prodigious sideburns of a similar salt and pepper disposition. My aimless wandering about the town becomes a waltz around his trajectory; and his around mine. A statue of Queen Victoria, a rather diminutive one, opposite the Bull Hotel, is bathed in ghostly green light, painted by lichen.

When I try to check in to my room at The Bull, they have me down for a booking two nights ago and all the other rooms are gone. I am temporarily allotted a room already booked out to someone else. The proprietor calls in on the room and then heads off to "try to sort something out". I am not under the creaking roof beams of the old inn like Sebald, but in an annexe at the back; a mini-flat with its own sitting room.

Uncertainty over the room and not eating since breakfast drive me to work, to think. It is the magical double movement again: I have a room, I do not have a room; I am hung in the superposition, generating until the wave collapses. 'My' little lounge assumes David Lynch-like qualities; it has a continuous ventilator hum, punctuated by occasional thumps from next door, and an enormous, tentacled dried-frond arrangement, a mirror, a landscape that is topological – a doughnut ring – and a table that Robert Wilson might have thrown off the set of one of his shows. Two identical prints of a bowl with a bonsai tree face each from the two longer walls of the narrow room, inert versions of the megalomaniac mirrors at Somerleyton Hall. The room fixes a relentless present. It is a smooth, aspirant non-place; Sebald's infinite present pinned between twin prints. All the crockery in the flat begins to vibrate, harmonising with the ventilation machine. Then the crockery stops and there is a new whirr; laundry perhaps.

I am reading a description of the Rendelsham Forest UFO flap; a little spooky given the poltergeist lounge accompaniment. The account comes from *Open Skies, Closed Minds* by Nick Pope, a former employee of the Ministry of Defence; I did finally find something in a charity shop.

It is 7.45pm and no one has come to tell me if I can stay or not; almost two hours since the proprietor called. I must check at reception... OK, I'm back. The Bull has transferred the other guests to another hotel, so I am safe! I have booked into the local wine bar for evening meal and live music of indeterminate provenance. The uncertainty is part of the 'ordeal': "taken from their beds... from their cars... while driving down a deserted road very late at night". And, of course, "missing time"; time abducted. Is that like Sebald's 'eternal present'? A history abducted by aliens, its causes and effects surgically replaced by conspiracies: a "hypnotically reinforced instruction not to remember"?

Everywhere on my walk I see the same phrase again and again and again: STAY CALM AND CARRY ON STAY CALM AND CARRY ON STAY CALM AND CARRY ON STAY CALM AND CARRY ON STAY CALM AND CARRY ON STAY CALM AND CARRY ON.

Pope refers to "the archaeologist Erich Von Däniken", which is rather like calling a Rolf Harris exhibition "major". There was a war in Heaven, it seems. I can believe that. Weird objects, circular and cylindrical, darted above city roofs. The entry for UFO in the Encyclopedia Britannica falls between "unicorn" and "unified field theory". That seems right, too; I am re-educating myself in the ufological basics. Pope writes that the term "foo fighters" originated in the Smokey Stover comics ("where there's foo there's fire"). I saw the science fiction author Brian Aldiss, no mean draughtsman, draw Smokey Stover's picture at a Cheltenham party held to launch a little pamphlet, *Naked In Cheltenham*, that the poet Adrian Mitchell had put together. Although I did not have a name for it at the time, I had spent the days of that Literary Festival on vodka-dérives with Adrian through Cheltenham streets, and the nights on the same streets trying to walk myself sober.

Just before his death I bumped into Adrian at a Laurie Anderson concert and he invited me to dinner, but I left it too late. Same old story. Aldiss, I remember, describing a story he wrote about a space craft set off into deep space with people from a dying Earth, great shields over its windows to protect the passengers from radiation; the craft had been travelling for generations when, still with no prospect of arrival at the promised new planet, a revolt breaks out and the shields are torn down to reveal that for all those years the ship has been orbiting the Earth. The story was very popular in Eastern Europe, but it works for any concentrated Spectacle; how do you know the landscape is not just a story of a landscape?

The Nordics "had a message... warnings about a nuclear Armageddon". Peace-Vikings from Outer Space. Maybe Sutton Hoo, to which tomorrow I intend to take a detour, will turn out to be a crash site. "The particular aliens whom he met were lying", "two red lights appeared on each side", floating dragon eyes, Mothman, "she pointed to her belly and then to the sky". Shon ap Shenkin rested against a tree to listen to a fairy melody, when the music finished the tree had died. Art appears to generate an 'eternal present', but drains time from action. The ventilator in the bathroom grinds on and on.

Susan Blackwood, having her *temporal* lobes stimulated on BBC 2's *Horizon*, felt that she was "physically manipulated by an entity she couldn't quite make out". Excuse me, Doctor Ideology? A letter crosses Pope's desk at the MOD: "I am writing to you with extraordinary news! There are aliens on my estate." Enclosed was a photograph of the galactic travellers: "the objects in the picture were crows". I see crows all the time, hear them often. "He heard a voice saying 'Prepare yourself – you are about to become the voice of the Interplanetary Parliament!'" How come the aliens never say anything about giving left cover to reformism?

Then the Rendelsham Forest story: 27.12.80, two patrolmen on the Bentwaters perimeter see bright lights, and a metallic triangle. Two days later "it" returns "as though it were an eye winking at you". Cheeky. Three objects, like stars but red, green, and blue, move about in angular motions, a light in "the midst of a strange circle of mist". The Mist in the military midst. The lights then transform into "a structured object" (following Levi-Strauss, it is a myth): midst ➤ mist ➤ myth. A myth 30 feet across the base and 20 feet high. Where it landed it left one-and-a-half-inch deep impressions in the ground; it must have been remarkably light, given the sandy soil. Wandering among the concrete remnants just outside the base perimeter, on the edge of Rendelsham Forest, I sank a foot into the ground.

The unnerving thing is that as you begin to sink – into shingle, Norwich roads, Underchalk, OB – you have no idea how deep you will go.

The craft has rainbow lights, like the crop watering machines. No record of an MOD response. "Local people had seen lights over the forest, but they were told to keep quiet... one couple who initially spoke to BUFORA had their property surrounded by barbed wire and MOVC signs forbidding entry." Others mentioned "unidentified shapes moving about inside the object", then "three creatures with large heads and dark eyes". From lights, to structured craft, to organisms. Light-structure-ideology.

As this tale of movement is slowed down, encumbered with ever more details, it becomes theological, faith-based and organic: "animals... went into a frenzy." (*The Terror*) "Rendelsham Forest became a myth." (Nick Pope).

"The flashing, pulsating lights in the streets were actually the rotating beams from Orford Ness Lighthouse six miles away." Orford Ness is a spacecraft!

That night a Russian rocket had re-entered the Earth's atmosphere; so was this all cover for a recovery mission? A crash site, literally? Were the lights seen by one unit of soldiers in fact the lights shone by another unit of the same soldiers? The lights in a spiral, hallucinating. "A highly advanced technology appeared in those Suffolk woods." "Intelligence... did not originate on earth."

On the TV they are advertising something called "KGB deals". Would they have considered "SS deals"?

Here in Woodbridge, the local estate agent is William H. Brown.

The question is: with what was given me, did I fulfil the promise? Never took it to the next level. I am leaving fragments; but where is the change from quantity to quality. The sound of heavy rain on the roof; the heatwave has broken. Softening flattened pheasants, rabbits, mice, hedgehogs, squirrels; I was tempted to pick up a pheasant's tail feather, today, to play Mephistopheles. What is hovering over my room now is a saucer of guilt.

Ever since it gave up any real hope of alien contact, ufology has been marinated in the fantasy of 'disclosure', the idea that in the emptiness left by its loss of faith, the state will step in and 'tell us the truth'; the fabulous promise of aliens landing on the White House lawn ends in minute exegeses of MOD phone logs. A vain hope; the state *long ago* owned up to its drives and desires; power no longer lies in the control of knowledge, but in the global promotion of a kind of *attention without content*.

The state does not really care what you know, because it took the 'know' out of knowing around the same time as it became transparent. This is why, despite the tolerant contempt of my colleagues in Wrights & Sites, I continue to monitor the offerings of occultists, ufologists and cryptozoologists; not because I expect any of them to discover anything, though they might, anyone might, but because they are the shadows of what we are missing. *UFO MATRIX* Vol. 2 Issue 1, purchased at a general store, believes it has unearthed a conspiracy: a copy of *Left At East Gate*, an account of the Rendelsham Forest UFO event, has been withdrawn from Suffolk Library Services, which, the magazine claims, is something that "only happens" when a book "has been deemed obscene or otherwise incredibly controversial". Er, no... sadly this kind of book-culling happens on a massive scale and is part of a dispersed strategy to destroy memory in general and public libraries in particular.

6.10.11

The man at my breakfast table says: "we went to Orford Ness – there's nothing there." With him and his wife, I discuss ancestry and how things disappear. Then I take a taxi to Sutton Hoo. It is no part of the Sebald narrative, but I want to see if I can use the place to devise subversive tactics for heritage visits.

I am a little early for opening time, but that gives me a few minutes to enjoy the 'Viking face' branding everywhere; very alien grey.

Eventually the place opens up and I check out the main information hub, quickly angered by its suggestion that because Celtic peoples did not have lords who were descended from the gods, it was fine for the Anglo-Saxons to colonise because their kings were divinely descended. What? Is this site run by The Racial Trust? By Anglish Heritage? According to Anglo-Saxon texts, the colonisers were not driven by the thrill of warfare, but by a desire to feast and to enjoy the tales of heroes; their motivation was beauty. Their power, while hierarchical, was OK because it was conditional on the affections of subjects. A kind of 'Terror', then, an early Society of the Spectacle. AND THEN there is no ship!!! He he! Because the timbers of the burial ship, the centre of everything at Sutton Hoo, were long ago eaten away by acids in the soil, leaving only a few rivets and timbers-shaped stains, the ship is essentially NOT THERE! This is a heritage site with a massive missing artefact at its centre: "the Anglo-Saxons have not disappeared, they have become invisible". I like the faceless mannequins in the display. I am strangely moved by the replica burial chamber of King Raedwald. Ivan had wanted to call his second son Raedwald, but had had to settle for Edwin; the middle name of my son, named after my maternal grandfather, the pattern maker.

I wander around the burial mounds enjoying being the first visitor there. I am impressed by the extent of the framing of these humps. Chain fence. Spot lighting. Hand cleanser. Viewing platform. Information board. Finger posts. And I begin to plan a heritage site consisting *only* of chain fences, spot lighting, hand cleanser, viewing platforms, information boards and finger posts.

I take a taxi to the edge of Rendelsham Forest. The driver tells me that her father was a band leader on the Isle of Man during summer seasons and that there was a "fairy bridge" there which whenever they crossed it they had to shout out "hello, fairies!" She tells me that the white deer in the forest signifies the coming of a new charismatic leader. "Not sure that Cameron fits that description", she says, "someone more like King Arthur." She tells me she has yet to see the white deer, though it would be magical for her, frustrated that it seems to mean so little to so many of those who have seen it. She points to the old oak trees lining the road explaining that they were planted as waymarkers for travellers on their way to the priories, "which were like hotels", she explains.

She is my angel: I realise that everything up till now has been prelude. The great walk is about to begin.

I follow the Rendelsham Forest UFO trail. This is *my* maze, *my* labyrinth; Somerleyton Hall and Dunwich Heath have been practice runs. On and on and still on it goes. I was expecting about half a mile of trail, but I have walked three miles at least and I still haven't reached the end; to be added on to the already long day's walking ahead. I am entirely alone on the Trail, except when a huge silvery figure cuts across my path, half blank head like the Sutton Hoo mannequins and half a Nordic Dan Dare. It is a trick of the light, but for a moment I see it very distinctly, the same size as the reared up Polar Bears at Somerleyton Hall, where our fellow visitors demonstratively recalled a recent Polar Bear attack on the tents of a group of adventuring young people, marvelling at the size of the animals and imagining the horror of finding oneself in their arms.

At the East Gate I had taken a photograph of a blemish in the road surface that I think looks remarkably like the head of a grey alien (*but which the horror writer Steve Duffy later more accurately describes as more like a pair of underpants*). The trees crackle and crack like the sounds of weapons being cocked. All the time I am on the lookout for the white deer. I walk so as not to be heard, like a member of an Auxiliary Unit Patrol. I find a clear space, a landing site, surely, so I mime entering the spacecraft and meeting my aliens. I take photographs of the sky directly above me.

At Site 3 there is a strange angel-string tangled everywhere, a woolly substance scattered about the forest floor. The Rendelsham Forest Centre was shut so unfortunately I do not have the leaflet (why am I not surprised?) to explain what is supposed to have happened at each of the numbered sites along the Trail. I make it up as I go along. Plus, there was a noticeboard at the start of the Trail that says how much the forest has changed since the 1980s – mostly replanted after the storm of 1987 – so, in a way, this Forest is another replica, a stand-in for something else missing. I relish the nonsense of it, the layers of simulacra, the disconnection that makes it all the more realunreal, detached and free floating.

There are three arrowed markers close together in a small clearing and I walk around them until I am dizzy, the layout swirls the brain, as if I were walking the *Uzumaki* swirls in St Edmund's Church, climbing the walls. I stupidly become nervous about unexpectedly coming upon the white deer, in a Cyclopean version, nine feet tall at the shoulder, a giant white hart standing in my path. This is unlikely as, due to the symmetrical planting of the coniferous trees, for most of time I can see up to half a mile through the forest.

To walk as quietly as possible, I swing my arms, creating a light footfall; still spooked, I turn and look over my shoulder and I know that I must appear in that moment exactly like the thing in the Patterson-Gimlin Bigfoot hoax footage, anxiously looking over my shoulder. Except for the pendulous breasts... Well...

This is my equivalent to Sebald lost on Dunwich Heath; not strictly lost, still on the Trail and following the markers, but feeling increasingly that, despite walking for an hour and a half, the posts are leading me further and further from where I want to return and deeper and deeper into a mental miasma. I disperse this by deploying my own internal Fog Investigation and Dispersal Operation (FIDO); a meditational version of the system deployed at Woodbridge Airfield during the Second World War, when up to 100,000 gallons of petrol were ignited every hour, to form sheets of flame for dispersing The Mist and bringing damaged bombers down safely.

I take my fire from two red dragonflies that accompany me, floating dragon eyes, through the sunlit part of the forest. The fire walks with me, inside and out; the burning moor and radioactive mists are parts of my extended organism now; the confusion evaporates, the posts become mere repetitions, I come to the Trail's end and depart the Forest, without having seen the deer. I step out for Hollesley Common, along a dusty track, glancing along a path branching to the left. Two small brown deer are feeding and, just beyond them, is the shining albedo of the white one! It bolts in a smear of silk and lightning, followed by the two brown ones, but I have seen it and it is enough. A few yards on, savouring the sighting of the milky vector, I startle a fox deep among the trees...

Follow animal tracks

ANIMALS ARE ALWAYS CLOSE. There are half a million spiders for every human in the UK; rats are never more than a few metres away. Even in towns and cities I have seen kingfishers, peregrine falcons, deer, parrots, pheasants, an otter and there are micro-scorpions to be found in the walls of UK ports, wallabies in Derbyshire and so on. Then there are those mythic creatures that you only catch in the corner of your eye; that turn into trees and benches as you approach them.

There are crocodiles in swimming pools, foxes in bedrooms, bears in sweet shops and herring gulls in chippies; and since the factory ships fished all the herring from the seas, those gull chicks born on cliffs starve to death in greater numbers every year. .

On my walks I have been attacked by a flock of Canada Geese in a field and by around one hundred Herring Gulls in a town square. These were two of the more imposing moments I have experienced of the continual flows above and around us. An era of increased synanthropisation, not to speak of escalating animurbanisation, has begun. Red foxes migrate northwards away from warmer temperatures, picking their way across K-Mart car parks and motorways and electrified fences. The pressure is on for animals to find their niche in recently-human-dominated places. Negotiations may sometimes become fraught. The LifeOnEarth/TopCat matrix may not hold forever. A change from the present paranoid separations may be on the cards. Mosquitos will take Florida again.

...then, crossing a wide, windy field, a disembodied voice speaks a few words to me and about two hundred black crows take off and wheel around me: alien theatre...

Bluster

WHICHEVER WAY THE WIND BLOWS, walk against it. As it changes, change your direction to meet it head to head.

...I take a wrong turn – a deceit on the part of the map – and add an extra two miles to my day's already distended walk. I cross fabulous purple moorland, raising a bright green game bird. I take a winding route through tunnels of the same green as the bird, around ponds, through a field of horses where I feel insecure and unwanted...

The right to more

WHAT ABOUT A RADICAL extension of the right to roam to factories and warehouses, military bases and power stations, to private gardens over a certain acreage?

This might help us to prepare for a culture of welcome and closeness necessary for the coming mass migrations north from the new deserts.

In 1998 Gregg and Gary of Lone Twin, for a performance called *Totem*, piloted a fallen telegraph pole in as straight a line as possible through the centre of the English city of Colchester. Unable to carry the pole alone, they were dependent on the help of others as they took it through shops, workplaces, homes and busy streets. We might profitably borrow Gregg and Gary's principle of 'activating social events through personal trials'.

...struggling to detect the true route of the path, working it out where it has been changed, allowed but not encouraged, I finally break out into a massive field, watered by a huge 400-metre-long metal arm that swings around a pivot. The wind batters me from head-on as I climb the rise of the field. At last, coming into Shottisham, relieved that I have not plunged forever through the thin roof of OB Underchalk, I coax a sick, blind rabbit out of the road and wonder if it might have been kinder to leave it to be run over.

All over Shottisham there are posters proclaiming the village's purchase of its own pub, but my landlady points out that the pub is now a limited company; the shares are held by those with money, rather than the whole village. The scheme had originated in a campaign to stop the pub's previous owner building homes on adjacent land – a move which some villagers would have appreciated, as it would have allowed younger villagers to stay in the village. I say to the landlady that I noticed, from documents on the village information board, that her husband is the chairman of the parish council. "He was till last week, when he resigned – it's a village..." She has an electrical fly swat called 'The Exterminator'.

After I tell her my story of an extravagantly staffed kitchen in a motel in Poland in 1989 and of how surprised my Polish colleagues were at the suggestion that without subsidy most of these people would lose their jobs, she says "it's happening here in the public sector". "Whenever one is imagining a bright future, the next disaster is just around the corner."

Through the window of The Sorrel Horse Inn, two red Mothman rear lights burn, fire everywhere; heatwave here, snow in Scotland. It is October the sixth, a week into my walk, and I have yet to wear my coat. Every day in a shirt. There is no such thing as nothing. For nothing is dark energy. And dark energy (nothing in motion) is taking over the universe. FIRE MIST HUNTING HERALDRY IDEAL ART OF LIVING/ LOVING

7.10.11

Over breakfast my landlady, whose main trade are the family members of prisoners at the nearby correctional facilities, tells me about riot training at Bentwaters. She recalls how frightened she was every time she went to the shops, having to walk along the wire fence where the UK police force conducted full-on training in the abandoned communal buildings of the old airbase.

> *"It is a war that must be waged constantly during peacetime*
> *to maintain the upper hand. It is a war that must be waged in*
> *secret."* Tony Collins

My landlady's husband, Mike, tells me what it was like living near the base as a youngster. In his bedroom he kept a piece of a Phantom that crashed in the fields near Sutton; the fire crews rushing to the scene had fallen foul of the Second World War tank traps. Mike talks of, later, living by the Woodbridge base, of the sounds of the thrusters on the fighter-bombers coming in low drowning out the TV and stinging his ears...

Rhythms

ONE OF THE RHYTHMS OF THE 'DÉRIVE' is made by walkers switching their attention between different foci, varying their distance from what they examine, oscillating from a collective gaze upon one another to a romantic gaze to the horizon. Falling for nothing, then for everything. While there is a mental aspect to this rhythmical looking, it is also a de- and re-composition of landscape. As the drift progresses, the rhythm of these switches can begin to take a compositional form; patterns emerge that then operate across the different scales.

> The Doctor: *"I can feel it. The turn of the Earth. The ground beneath our feet is spinning at a thousand miles an hour, the entire planet is hurtling around the sun at sixty-seven thousand miles an hour, and I can feel it. We're falling through space, you and me, clinging to the skin of this tiny little world..."*

...of Lightnings taking off to intercept Soviet aircraft noseying around: "cat and mouse, you could learn a lot". He tells me of his work in Pershore at a facility where they created light conditions "from bright sunlight to starlight". "At the infra-red end", he says "a lot of our light comes from the stars." I ask him who constructed this technology and he says "MOD". We exchange tales of theatre lighting. He once did the sound effects for a village pantomime on a reel-to-reel and missed his cue; an actress was to bend her back and a great creaking sound to result. She waited to bend, but no sound would come. When I mention to Mike the round-towered churches I passed, he says there are plans to use them for improving rural broadband.

Walking this morning I am struck that the landscape that Sebald describes as so completely militarised, with guarded gates and barracks down every turning, is not like that now. Many of the air bases are closed and I see little sign of military activity, but I know it is there because everybody keeps telling me about it; like the rich at the end of their drives, the military seems increasingly reticent on its own ground. But then, if it "must be waged in secrecy" why would it be any different?

I see herons overhead. Then a black deer, antlered, takes off in the field to the left of me. Racing across the ground, it draws a diagonal from corner to corner of the field's rectangle, crossing the road a hundred yards up ahead and slices into a field to the right, symmetrically again, and finally disappears; into an ideal field, presumably. I see fake hawks above the crops on flexible poles, bending in the wind.

My path begins to follow a line of Martello towers towards the coast and I finally reach the edge of the crucible, a great lip of stone beach. I am part of it now. Climbing onto Shingle Street I picture the rumoured sheets of fire: here, so the stories go, a German mini-invasion (or bungled Allied rehearsal) was incinerated by burning gas jets from submarine pipes. I wonder if there could have been confusion with the fog dispersal at Woodbridge? Or maybe they used the same technology here?

"Shingle Street": strange that I should have *invented* that name as the title for my first community jazz oratorio with Stroud Community Choir, writing lyrics based on interviews with the choir members, the music composed by Pete Rosser, and the late Karen Debonnaire directing and conducting (Karen who had grown up on the Bell Green council estate where my Gran and Grandad had lived, where on Sundays we would visit and I would eat mince pies with almost no mince washed down with lukewarm milk from a fridgeless larder, and then, escaping family claustrophobia, would be swiftly identified and punished by the local gangs. Karen's daughter Eilidh is now on tour with our adaptation of *David Copperfield*. "Our first TNT Theatre baby", Paul says.) I had no idea at the time that there was a real Shingle Street, and now I am upon it, treading across its shingle, each stone a grey fist, the gaps opening and grasping at my ankles. I am following a trail of white shells that leads me away from the burning sea, over stones clicking like damaged knuckles, and up to a house with sculptures and a text that reads: AND WE ARE PUT ON EARTH A LITTLE SPACE – THAT WE MAY LEARN TO BEAR THE BEAMS OF LOVE. The quotation is from *The Little Black Boy* by William Blake, a poem about the searing heat of god. (Did the sculptor get this text via its quotation by Thomas Merton?) Mystical inferno, spiritual incineration. Love that burns flesh. Love that turns bones to ash as white as deer and leaves soil stained in the shape of the sun. Is that what the MOD was up to at Pershore? I have heard of light being slowed under laboratory conditions, even standing still. And if they stopped light then, Einstein permitting, they stopped time too. An eternal present, in an MOD lab.

At one of my B&Bs a guest told me of a plan to give shepherds remote controlled model-planes, they meant drones, to replace their sheep dogs.

As I leave Shingle Street a woman stops her car and asks me if I have seen an Afghan hound. No, I haven't. She drives off towards Hollesley. I meet a man just back from the beach and we talk for half an hour or so. He is a trickster, an elf, one of the fairy people; he wears a pork pie hat, his teeth are varied shades of yellow and he speaks elliptically, grinning and jesting, and then delivering little sniping stabs: "you're young, well fed... do you work for the government? You're a think tank! Tinker, Tailor, Soldier, Spy, all that time in those third rate boarding houses... are you running away from your creditors? I was a bank manager and solicitor, but look at me now! I'm a broken man inside! When you come to live in a village put it about that you're bone idle, slightly retarded, that it runs in the family on the father's side, that the women are quite industrious, but that your marriage is only for the purposes of satisfying your physical needs.... the problem is: neighbours. I've been thinking about how to categorise them: hostile!"

The grinning elf lists the subjects for conversation in a village: "moles, silage, septic tanks and backache... and then a deadly silence. Occasionally someone will ask: 'is Harold Wilson still Prime Minister?'" "And is the pound still in his pocket?" I ask. A deadly silence. It is code. He is giving me the nod. "When I came here twenty years ago my wife said 'we musn't vegetate', so I would buy up bits of land, bogs really, nobody wanted them. But now they do; and you find you have neighbours coming round to say did you know that their grandfather put a line of posts across that bit of land you think you own and let's go and have a look… (he mimes tripping over a post) … 'there you are!' Have you seen the new £20 note? They asked Mervyn King about the cost of the ink – he said they're only going to print it on one side."

At times I think he might be mad, so intense is his slipperiness; pulling all sense apart. I wonder if he's pumping me for information. He gets plenty, but I'm putting a shifty spin on it, like he does to his. He is wonderful. He describes his walks as "aimless". When I first meet him, I greet him, to his confusion, with "a woman's lost an Afghan". And as I walk away from him now, exhausted from thirty minutes of unrelenting comic fencing, I realise that he must have thought I meant a person from Afghanistan, and I wonder why on earth that would be his first thought.

The dog woman returns and says to me "she's got him" and I see another woman a field away leading the hound out of the dunes. The two women set off in separate cars, the Afghan in the back of one. The second woman stops her car and asks: "Do you know who owns the sheep there? One of them is on its back." I pass a flattened snake on the road, I add it to my flat fox, flat squirrel, flat rabbit, flat gull. I walk through the complex of prisons at Hollesley Bay, for a while in step with prisoners moving from one building to another; I came far too close to this walk, once.

Myths, freed from imitation, are still useful, for they show us to ourselves: suspended above a void, reaching out for the lip of the abyss, all of us, sustained, to the margins; Scottie hanging from the gutter in *Vertigo*, L.B. Jefferies from the window ledge in *Rear Window*…

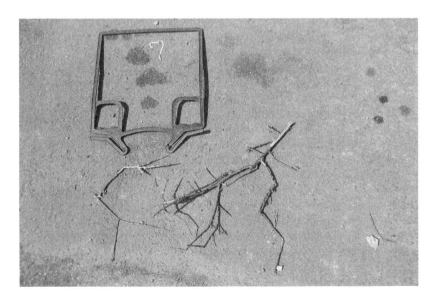

Psychogeography

THERE IS A *deep autotopographical* walking (to adapt terms from Dee Heddon and Nick Papadimitriou) in which autobiography or psychological transformation and crisis are key strands in the weaves around the route. There is no therapeutic guarantee here; what a walk tends to do is to set things in motion, but their eventual trajectory will be determined by your own choices and interventions, by others, by terrains and by accidents.

...I am glad to pass the 'Out Of Bounds' sign without having to take any notice of it; a mark of the unevenness of borders and mobilities.

When I taught poetry to the prisoners in Horfield Jail I was always deeply relieved when the guards let me out.

I thought I could detect among the modern buildings and steel fences of Hollesley Prison, older structures that might have been parts of the forced labour colony here in the 1930s. I pass fields of harvested onions. Up ahead lines of prisoners head off among the furrows to work.

In the pub at Butley there is a framed photograph of a downed German bomber, locals posing around it bearing weapons. In a lay-by, beside a child's drawing of a Cthulhu-like monster, is a letter from a landlord, a farm owner, informing a tenant that they have not paid their rent on time and asking how they intend to make up the arrears.

Reaching Orford, I take afternoon tea in the Riverside Tearoom, surprised at how visible the research buildings on the Ness are from the Quay; impressed at the invisible forces (D notices, OSA, and so on) that once kept such places largely unspoken of.

Conscientiously I follow Sebald's text to the Castle, but, o my god, the man with the plastic bags from Woodbridge is waiting for me there. I can tell that he notices me; a flicker that he conceals. I try to pretend that I do not recognise him. Now, we are both weaving round the Castle pretending not to recognise each other. If my paranoia was any more than a simple aesthetic ploy for the purposes of mythogeographical hyper-sensitisation I might begin to wonder at some of my other encounters since Sizewell.

I retreat to The Jolly Sailor and check in. This is where the researchers on the Ness drank together. What secrets were whispered in my room? I go down to the bar for a few pints and dinner. Was it difficult for the scientists to discipline themselves not to speak of their work while socialising, while drinking? Did they mumble hypotheses across their beers? What presence if any did the Soviets have in the town, in the Jolly Sailor even? Did they send mermen? Did they ever turn anyone? How worried were the security services by the Communist presence at nearby Leiston? Why no protests from there; only, ineffectively, from the 'ultra-leftist' Committee of 100? Maybe the Soviets had a more complicated agenda? The Ness had been declared vulnerable to security breaches by the British intelligence services; so perhaps the Soviets were keen to keep the research here rather than disrupt it? I recall Mike's comments earlier in the day about the infractions of Soviet aircraft as being opportunities to learn about them… o my lord, the strange-looking man with the plastic bags from Woodbridge has now turned up in the bar of The Jolly Sailor and settles down at the next table. O, and now he jumps up, abandoning his three large bags… do I… ah, no, he's back again… we continue to pretend not to notice each other.

Sebald was wrong about melancholia; fearing that a person so depressed might bring about the end of the world. Melancholia and depression bring on a painful creativity, repair and interweaving. It is paranoia that will end the world; excitedly, in both thrilling self-pity and fear, fuelled by a belief in special persecutions and in an everything-threat which must be destroyed.

(Later I get to see Lars Von Trier's film. It is a remake of *Cloverfield*, but instead of the monster it is the bourgeoisie that runs rampant, under the path of a 'rogue' blue planet that first passes by the Earth and then spirals, hypnotised by gravity, back into it.)

I am chatting, very enjoyably, with a friendly couple from Colchester, Cath and Mike, but as 'conventional walkers' there is a cut-off point, and they are pumping me for information, and I do not leave enough space or make the proper invitations to let them explain themselves, though they do describe Mersea Island, mentioned by my angelic taxi driver yesterday. Cath and Mike tell me how they had to time their visits according to the tides otherwise the road across to the island would be covered by water.

The man with the plastic bags polishes off a main course and orders the same again. A hairy man certainly, the man with the plastic bags may also be a merman.

After its first escape, the Orford merman returned, of its own 'free will', and swam back into the nets. The fantasy about the 'other' is that it really wants to be subservient, but that its 'nature' spoils things. The merman eventually swam off never to return.

On the local TV news there is an account of a car bursting through the barriers by the Southwold lifeboat office and plunging into the Blyth. The elderly driver is drowned; I worry about my encounter with the old silk man: was it a countdown I had not recognised? Earlier today, I passed a van with a picture of a goldfish and a slogan: "He doesn't have a scale problem. Do you?" Is David Icke doing home visits? I saw another insect sculpture, just off the road on the way into Orford. As if I had been here before. As if Mum had not died and I had come here in the summer.

8.10.11

I am up early, keen not to miss the first boat onto Orford Ness. It is a short trip to emptiness. Stepping ashore, I am mindful that this is where they tested the MAD gamble and exercised a trigger finger on the end of the world...

Walk to the ends of the earth

WALK AS IF THE APOCALYPSE has been under way for some time. It has.

...I set off towards AN/FPS-95, System 441a, Cobra Mist. The other visitors head off in the opposite direction, towards the weapons labs. A flock lines up to face me, fifty sheep stand abreast. I walk two miles down a concrete road. There is something intensely ascetic, meditational even, about concrete roads. For fifteen years this place, this nature reserve, was a major player in maintaining the UK's nuclear deterrent. Here they tested the ballistics of the bombs and the reliability of the trigger mechanisms. Without reliability there was no real deterrent, and the enemy had to know how reliable it was, so maybe the Ness's intelligence vulnerability was useful, intentional even. Bombs, 'duds', were dropped, while tracked by operators using steerable helical aerials mounted on the trials building. To the naked eye, even with an aircraft at 40,000 feet, gleaming white in a blue sky, the open bomb bay doors and the orange painted weapon were all visible. Bombs were 'cans of tomatoes'. The weapon, a Yellow Sun, solar fire, was released well before it was overhead, to the eye far too early, making a rumbling sound as its blunt nose buffeted the air, then a huge splash a quarter of a mile offshore. No nuclear materials were ever on the Ness; always substituted with 'a placebo'... this may not be entirely true. The training crews of the V bombers knew there was little chance of surviving a real raid; they were suicide bombers. Scimitars were also nuclear-armed; top secret until all the details turned up in an issue of the *Eagle* comic. No point in a deterrent unless the enemy knows precisely what it is; there is little room for misunderstanding in nuclear chess.

First off the boat, I had marched this way in the hope of walking solitarily across the two miles to the remnants of Cobra Mist, remembering how being alone had affected my experience of the wards, operating theatre, cinema and morgue of the German underground hospital beneath Guernsey. And why, as a teenager, I would sneak into the grounds of stately homes and heritage sites after they were closed; not to vandalise or steal, but to experience, to feel, because a curtain was pulled back in these places after the visitors and staff were gone. The places behaved differently on their own; but you had to sneak up on them.

I am less personally unnerved than I was under Guernsey; the dispiriting is general this time. The distant, silent pylons, thin as cotton thread, pin the grey reedy grasses to the grey skies. This is a plane irradiated. I know that the shingle is alive with rare species and that the greys and browns are just as much signs of vibrancy as the greens and yellows on the Orford shore, the brochure says so; but it is all a show, all set aside, things turned out differently on the spit, hinged inadequately below Aldeburgh the land flapped about in history for a while and then went limp. In this displaced place time timed out, the Russians did not read the Eagle, the back channels were not used in '62, the enemy was not empathised with, the Cuban Missile baby was never born. I did not walk this walk. The animals act their parts, playing dead, everything puts on a play of silence but the wind. I arrive at a clumsily metaphorical bridge.

Beyond the cheap movie space station of the now silent, stilted Foreign Office funded, BBC World Service transmitter, little remains of Cobra Mist; a dim spread upon the ground like the dusty spectre left by a bird crashing into a window pane. The very thinness of the pylons, barely visible against the grey skies, and the faint shadows of the ground plan all evoke the massive invisible energy resources that once powered a fan of antennae spread across more than one hundred and thirty acres, with a giant broadcast signal of 10 megawatts, designed to detect missile activity two thousand miles away.

But Cobra Mist was not empathetic to its enemies; it was haunted by the ghost of General Curtis LeMay, the architect of a strategic bombing campaign responsible for the destruction of 40% of residential districts in sixty-six Japanese cities and advocate of a bombing of Soviet missile sites in Cuba in 1962 that would have begun a nuclear exchange; his spectre operated as an organising force among the various active elements hung from the eighteen strings of antennae radiating out from the centre on the eastern shore and within the reflective mesh hung beneath them. Wherever the antennae were 'pointed', they found missile launches everywhere. Each time they turned on the system, the LeMay possession started a war. The System was never used operationally, and, closed after months of tests, at a final cost of $150 million (almost one billion of today's dollars). Having paid my respects to its dubious corpse, I make my way back across the island towards the remnants of the Atomic Weapons Research Establishment. Three brown hares go skittering away across the shingle; I had mistaken them for rusty ordnance.

The railings around the Bomb Ballistics building are tuned to C major.

The Lighthouse will be allowed to crumble into the sea.

The pagodas strike me as elegant, their shapes designed to absorb blast. I cannot get admittance to them because they are "too dangerous", though a party who have paid extra is visiting them. Rent; even here. There is a very powerful

atmosphere at the entrance to AWRE Laboratory One, an ambience of torn souls and troubled thoughts...

Atmospheres

On the various walks I have participated in, I have felt some things, experienced some atmospheres, very strongly. Sometimes I have felt similar things in very different spaces that might yet be connected, not by cause and effect but by shape and mythogeometry.

Here is my account of coming upon a shape of dread, a recently redundant church at a remote Devon crossroads. We stumbled upon it during a *Taxi to Westwood and Featureless* drift sometime around 2001; thanks to a so-called 'catapult' that involved us being driven at four in the morning, blindfold, by a taxi driver who we had paid with a couple of notes and asked to drop us somewhere we were unlikely to recognise:

> the crossroads with the old red telephone box and adverts
> for bus services and an orchestral concert in Exmouth, the
> vintage Jaguar dealers, the house, the bus shelter like a mossed
> shell the animal gone but still useful, and then the church
> with a 'for sale' sign leaning, its metal spike raw and exposed,
> against the gate. Simon walked ahead, up the suspiciously
> grassy path, past a large, ominous, garish bush, disappearing
> like Kim Novak. Mary, Amy and I followed. I began to feel that
> feeling. The purple flowers and the not quite right crosses on
> the ridges of the church roof in the not quite right light. Amy
> spotted a large black slug that was sliding itself beside the
> gravestones of the Sluggetts family. In the porch, tucked into
> the eaves, Simon found fragments of the electoral register;
> names and addresses. There was nothing on the noticeboards.
> Was it already de-consecrated? How can they do that when
> the dead are still here? By what authority? Another purple
> flowering bush humming like a radio, full of bees. Grapes in
> stone on the porch. 'Blue apples.' Honey. Gold. Is it so easy to
> turn off the energy of this place? Close it down, just like that?
> Like the grid of pylons could be turned off; but with what
> consequences for the dead?

How old is this site of death, stone and honey? And how many things have been worshipped here? By turning it off, what is blacked out? What disorder, what incivility to corpses? Turning back just before the gate and the 'for sale' sign; the purple bush seems to have darkened now; even more sweet, libidinous and looming. It has closed over the path, shutting something off. Something we haven't seen yet: uncanny, unhomely – because there is the possibility now; the shutting down of orthodoxy is the opening of 'everything else'. It has the same attraction as lanes turning off into who knows what? This is a place of Pan-ic – the pattern of place and atmosphere described by those who recount a sudden experience of terror (or Pan-ic) at the presence of everything but themselves, at the presence of the possibility of everything. This is like the woods where every way looks like every other. Later, in woods, we walk for maybe thirty minutes or more through unchanging terrain; not fear, but the imaginary possibility of walking in circles.

I know from race-walking that one of my feet is set in the ankle at a wider angle than the other. I've read Stephen King's *The Girl Who Loved Tom Gordon* – a girl lost in a forest. I've been lost in one for long hours as a child. A potent absurdity: the church, locked, unused, the paths being retaken by grass. The suicide of orthodoxy has opened the (obscure) paths to everything (else). Henry Ford and Herr Diesel, General Motors and Dunlop are gods here. History not two thousand, but less than a hundred years old, taking the orientalist form of Jaguars, E-Types, and their struggle for immortality against rust. The slug god, huge and a treacly black, creeps over the stones of a gelatinous family of former human matter in the ground. A god that puckers to the human touch. An intelligence unlike that of a father, but like everything. The empty church: looking so regular, except in the tell-tale details. This feeling has been described by the Danish philosopher:

"there is peace and repose; but at the same time something different, which is not dissension or strife, for there is nothing to strive with. What is it then? Nothing. But what effect does nothing produce? It begets dread... the reflex of freedom within itself at the thought of

its own possibility... the alarming possibility of being able... What it is he is able to do, of that he has no conception... There is only the possibility of being able, as a heightened expression of dread... he loves it and flees from it... the infinite possibility, which does not tempt like a definite choice, but alarms and fascinates with sweet anxiety."

There is a tendency to mistake this uncanny energy for ominous aggression, to fear it; in his youth the writer Arthur Machen encountered its giant scale in the Welsh valleys around Caerleon, but could only, and, he admitted, unsatisfactorily (if famously) transform and betray it into horror in his *The Great God Pan*. But it is much more to do with fear of a relationship with the fearsome immensity of everything than with the fearful incarnation of an ancient god.

...this is a space unphotographable. As part of its construction, huge shingle abutments were bulldozed into place; they looked like burial mounds to Sebald. I had seen their equivalents at Sutton Hoo.

Many of those who worked on the Ness never understood the function or meaning of the work they did. Chapman Pincher, the spook journalist, hung about on the Quay trying to buy information; he was told that they were developing radiation-free cattle. After the 1953 floods flame-throwers were used to incinerate the drowned cows.

Old bangers were use to travel about in the salty winds of the Ness, driven down to their wheel rims and then bulldozed into the shingle. A locomotive was left to rust away in the salt marsh.

Along the North Sea shoreline orange bricks have been rubbed into lozenges. I wander through the remains of fences, metal pylons, concrete circles, twisted rust-red boilers and lighting towers. It feels as if I have special permission to mooch around on location during the shooting of *Quatermass II*. I wonder how much its writer, Nigel Kneale, knew of this place? And whether all the monsters, mermen, dragons and winged crocodiles were cover stories for what went on here, or whether what went on here was cover for the monsters.

Sizewell, Orford Ness and Dunwich: all parts of one complex for the production of Cthulhu, property and rent. Perhaps it is all just too abject and agreeable now. Every now and then – like the fountains at Lowestoft – the buildings should erupt, not with water but with a great sheet of FIDO flame. I lie on the shingle and write for an hour; when I get up and return to the path I notice the sign:

```
┌─────────────────────────────────────────┐
│                                          │
│      THE  NATIONAL  TRUST                │
│                                          │
│            DANGER                        │
│                                          │
│      UNEXPLODED  ORDNANCE                │
│                                          │
│  PLEASE  KEEP  TO  THE  VISITOR  ROUTE   │
│                                          │
└─────────────────────────────────────────┘
```

and recall how my mate Nick and me, kids, had dug up an anti-aircraft shell on
a building site, trying to get it to go off by throwing it against an electricity sub-
station wall. Failing that, we took it to his Dad, a former rear gunner in bombers. He
made us return it to where we found it – suspended above a void, now, reaching out
for the lip of the abyss – while he called the bomb squad. I will try to practise that
careful, gentle walk back to the building site.

This potent landscape is what brought me here and it does not disappoint me.
However, I suspect there is not the same gradation of affect for me as for Sebald;
his description of the strangeness has drawn me here. But it is a strangeness that I
find everywhere.

The everyday is a theatre of the absurd and Orford Ness with its extermination
cathedrals and concrete roads to possessed backscatter radar and cameras obscura
are part of a performance I have attended before; of a piece with the military
holiday everyday entanglement everywhere.

I no longer feel any desire to linger. I have looked and touched and lain down
and crawled and written and thought and gathered, but I have not felt the urge
to savour. Just as at Dachau Concentration Camp Memorial Site I am keeping
away from other visitors; in the face of mass extermination I feel no attraction to
personalise, but instead to wrestle with what it is in abstraction.

I catch the boat back to Orford. In an unaffected little building full of books,
at the bottom of a garden packed with hens, a cockerel and tiny chicks, I buy *The
Blood of October* by David Lippincott: "an Indian Summer... most oppressive in
memory... To an already nervous and unsettled country, this peculiarly added one
more degree of uneasiness". In Orford church I kneel by the font to meet the gaze
of the stone 'hairy man'.

Dinner in the bar. The plummy man who was earlier selling mediocre landscapes
on the main drag is now loudly extolling the virtues of Enoch Powell. I realise
that I have not seen a black person since Lowestoft... o, except that I walked with
black prisoners in Hollesley Bay. That's all right then. In comes the BBC's Political

Correspondent Nick Robinson (Blue Robbo) and I realise that it is time to retire to my room, with a double scotch from the bar.

The Quest Channel is airing *Future Weapons*, boosting an upgrade of the A1ocv as if it were a new sports car. It can fire missiles from 15,000 feet with the help of 'new' infra-red technology; a weapon for the Cold War European theatre, at least a generation out of date. It will not win hearts and minds like an army fighting street by street that does not torture, abuse or rape the civilians. A USAF trainer brags about seeing what brand of cigarette his target is smoking - but he can never offer her one.

9.10.11

I am awake at 4am. The first dream I remember since beginning the walk: I have come from the lobby of a building, I am acting self-importantly. Some business acquaintance, perhaps annoyed, leaves and the dream changes to a park where a woman, someone I recognise but do not know well, perhaps Helen who leads walks at West Town Farm, is storytelling. She begins a new story, a large crowd gathers, but acrid smoke begins to billow around her... uh, for one moment I thought I was writing this down in the dream, but I am not, I'm real, I can hear the heavy rain outside... The smoke makes her and many in the audience cough. I am lying on the grass, low enough to escape the noxious fumes. I say "get low" and then I, selfishly, think: 'now they'll breathe up all the fresh air down here'. A cart or carriage drawn by a single horse passes by and a mechanical vehicle with metal jaws snarls at the horse. The operator opens the jaws of the digger and then turns the vehicle up a small road beside a building where two other machines are at work. There is a short altercation between the drivers and the machine with the jaws begins to topple. One of the other machines moves and touches this first machine with its digger arm so that it tips right over, crashing onto the main road. I say to the people in the crowd "now, there'll be a punch up" (it feels stale, as if I have already said this line earlier in the dream). The operator who tipped the machine over approaches angrily, he is dressed in yellow overalls: "that'll teach you, you chicken!" His workmate, after releasing a lever, pulls the main body of the prone machine off the body of its operator. The angry yellow-overalled man says: "you're lucky he's here to..." and then his voice breaks and he begins to cry. I can only see from the side, but there are large patches of blood on the injured man's lumberjack shirt. He does not move. I think he will die – I wake up. The rain outside is falling more heavily and I mine my room for significant layers of text. In the *East Anglian Magazine* of March 1956 there is a story about the inscription on "a 506-year-old Essex gravestone", which eluded all attempts to identify its location until the whole thing was traced back to a story in the *Toronto Times* of 1942, "a hoax which caught on through the circumstances of war":

> "When pictures look alive with movements free,
> When ships like fishes sail beneath the sea,
> When man outstripping birds can scan the sky,
> Then half the world deep drenched in blood will be."

People & Places: an actor, a chef, the High Sheriff and one hundred pages of Property and Rent.

I start my walk early, bypassing the villages of Sudbourne and Iken, once cleared of people for practice tank battles. On the Sudbourne estate I am subjected to the same level of surveillance as I was around Sizewell. Spotted by his lordship from the top of a field, he pointedly drives past a while later towards the house and soon I have a Land Rover and gamekeeper keeping pace with me on a parallel track through a succession of fields. Walking across the estate takes an hour or more. It is big. And all the while I am accompanied.

Perhaps this is where Grandad was a loader for the shoot. Presumably they think I am after a grouse or pheasant. A crowd of the birds gather near cages by the Decoy Wood which I enter and pass out of sight; stepping to the side of what is real.

I spend much of the day walking alone in woods. I ponder the great controversy over the Coalition Government's attempt to sell off the forests and the subsequent backlash; but wonder if it is the *idea* of forest, the oak tree, the national *symbols* that are defended, rather than the trees themselves; over-managed, de-populated and without spontaneity. Things crop up again: William H. Brown estate agents, William Brown base commander at Bentwaters. I am forced to think again, again and again, of the comrade I abandoned. I arrive eventually, after a long walk along a perimeter fence, passing skeletal baseball bleachers, at the security checkpoint for Bentwaters Park, an industrial estate now, site of the old air base, where once they held the operational power to start the end of everything.

The guard invites me into his van and drives me round to the Bentwaters Cold War Museum where I am welcomed by Errol who passes me on to Alan. The museum is closed, but a large number of the volunteers are on site, working on parts of aircraft in various states of decay.

The museum is housed in what was the command and control centre of the Bentwaters base. Alan takes me through the decontamination procedure: disposing of contaminated clothes, showering and scrubbing, changing into a fit-all set of new clothes. I am unsure whether the orange light that bathes the shower section is entirely 'authentic'. Maybe apocalyptic reality is just like it is in the movies. Alan says: "it's not just about missiles and bombs", by which he means that the museum is also about the people who worked here. There is not much evidence of them.

"I like Americans, but they are paranoid", he says, and takes me into a room full of telephone exchange equipment. The Americans put all their external communications through their own electronic filters. The next room contains a machine for decontaminating "dirty air" from a poisoned Suffolk. The assumption was that the Soviets would use chemical and biological as well as nuclear weapons. An old handwritten sign on a machine: "handle like eggs".

I look at many, many, many, many artefacts, mostly fascinating and extraordinary: notably the documentation of the Tigers Meet which began as a social get-together of units of different nations' air forces and span off into recreational flying, the participants adding a tiger to their badges, (there is a photo of a woman in a tiger skin bikini at one of their gatherings; "booze ups", says Alan), but there was an accident, during some informal flying together wings touched;

there were attempts to cover it up (what weapons were being carried?). Senior commanders stepped in, but rather than close down Tigers Meet, the commanders franchised it, encouraging "inter-operationality", so what began as fun became an operational structure: a classic Deleuzo-Guattarian 'war machine', all things creative only losing their last ounce of life in the hands of the military hierarchy.

Alan shows me a shell from an A10's 'Gatling Gun' (same plane as on TV last night; everything weaves so tightly now that it takes an effort to feel surprised). It is huge. Positioned and fixed at the front of the aircraft, the pilot points the plane to aim the weapon. The shell is, in its operational state, tipped with depleted uranium, and Alan becomes very animated about this: "take your head off five yards away or you die of the radiation!" It can cut through the skin of a tank.

The reinforced concrete of the command centre, capable of melting diamond-tipped drills, was always unlikely to survive a direct nuclear strike; at best it might have kept the fallout at bay for a while. They assumed that it might stay operational for three weeks; after that the staff would shoot themselves or open the doors to find out what was left. Alan's phrase for nuclear war is "if things got funky".

I ask about security around the perimeter and he describes how in Cold War days he and other aircraft enthusiasts would gather at a spot outside the fence near the church of St John the Baptist: "the Americans called it 'Commie Corner'". He would photograph the planes coming in and out: "some of the Americans would come and speak to us, give us candy, badges. Others would call us 'commies' and 'wankers'." Alan says the security guards gave you no trouble, unless you were a protestor; then they would let you break in just far enough to excuse setting a dog on you.

Many of the volunteers around the Cold War museum wear incomplete military uniforms. I wonder at their motivations; there is nothing overtly fascistic or ultra-militaristic about them, they are enthusiasts, but they get excited about the toolkit of killing. There are no victims on display. This is a Museum of Something That Never Happened; an iconic mythogeographical site. The most evocative expression of the missing artefact – annihilation – at the centre of the site is its ringing by faceless dummies in flying suits and uniforms. There was no battle in Europe.

The guys at the Cold War Museum, generous to a fault, are unable to dialogue with me, so intense is their focus on the *things* they have brought into a structure around nothing; the more they repair their planes the less they have.

Alan points to newspaper cuttings of the Rendelsham UFO flap: "Bollocks, I think it is". But Rory has a theory: it was a bungled practice exercise for rescuing the Apollo capsule, hence all the lights in the forest, a triangular craft bobbing about in the trees and large-headed occupants. A story of a UFO flap avoided the embarrassment of admitting that they dropped an Apollo.

Rory takes me into the most secure rooms in the base, demonstrating a 'serving hatch' for passing orders into the holey of holeys. This is where they held the war plans, guarded at all times by two armed officers; ready to shoot each other. In the event of exercises (theatre) or if "things got funky" (theatre, again) the necessary maps were retrieved from a vault and information from these was passed up to the senior officers in a command room above, separated by a glass panel from 'The Pit'.

Rory takes me down into 'The Pit'; it comprises two banks of telephones and a wall of 'write and wipe' boards listing all the operational units, and the individual pilots with various statuses against their names: loading weapons, fuelling, taking off, and so on. The task of the base was to get these pilots into the air and above the battlefield in Germany. Most of the planes were A10s; tank killers. After any mission, aircraft were decontaminated and disarmed. Rory says the strange concrete structures I had seen behind the guard post at East Gate were for disarming aircraft on landing; in case a weapon was accidentally discharged the aircraft were pointed at the structure, like the Ness pagodas they were designed to soak up impact.

The only evidence of anti-nuclear resistance in the museum are a few artefacts in a small case devoted to Civil Defence.

I am shown models of Vampires and a version of the Sabre, both planes my Dad flew, the latter at speed towards East German airspace, before banking away sharply, with the intention of turning on their radar. Theatre. Rory points at a model Starfighter – "the flying coffin" – and describes it as "basically a rocket"; a tank powered by rockets; so the blotchy man's experiments in Suffolk ditches did bear fruit.

The "crème de la crème" at Bentwaters were the 'Aggressors'; their job was to train pilots to think themselves inside the heads of Russian fighter pilots, to anticipate their enemies' choices in combat. To get inside the minds of the Russian pilots. These US superpilots created a Little Russia, ate Russian food, spoke in Russian to each other, decorated their quarters with Russian artefacts. An anomalous domain within an anomalous domain. A Russia within a USA within a UK. Dolls within dolls. "Empathise with your enemy." Robert McNamara's Lesson #1.

For two hours or more, with intense passion and huge generosity, the volunteers of BCWM have installed in me the structure of their Cold War museum; from the decontamination unit just below my skin, dirty air filters for my lungs, The Pit in my guts, the serving hatch to my criticism, and at the centre of me the thing that never happened. These guys are real alchemists, my visit a working: calling into being a hollowness at the middle of me...

Alchemical crossing

WHEN USING A 'ZEBRA CROSSING' with a large group of people, rehearse everybody up to shout "Albedo!" when they step on the white segments and "Nigredo!" when they step on the black segments. This will evoke the putrefaction of matter and call out the inner fire that is found within it. To symbolise the wedding or crossing of the two, particularly if you are lucky enough to have pink pavement tactiles at each end of the striped crossing, all yell out "Rubedo!" on reaching the 'other side'.

... allowing passion and generosity to irradiate out. They have taught me how to not be. I thank them profusely; them and me only dimly aware of what they have done. I walk the broad roads of the base back towards the gate, numb inside and vibrating on every edge; walking a plane. Pass a fallen sign to "Hush House"; that is what I am now. Shhh. The different layers shifting like the blades of a turbine freed to move independently of each other. The outer layer of the housing, hushed. I see the white domed UFO, across the base; it is certainly not Sizewell B, not there. The security guard explains that it is a bio-fuel processor: "we call it Sizewell C and a half".

I walk to Wickham Market station; I am a hovercraft floating just above the dusty track, newly lightened by losing my centre. I know that life is not hidden within, but on every layer, because I saw it. For when I said: "That's it". Well. It was not. After Mum's last breath my Dad, who my sister and I, seeing how things were moving, had called into the bedroom, made a strange gesture. Perhaps something from one of his freemasonic rituals. With his finger he made a shape across Mum's body, a triangle, like the pattern of a V bomber or a cross joined at the tips, something subtle and esoteric, perhaps, or maybe something jumbled by his dementia. Mum gently spasmed, a sort of shudder and was still in a final way. But it did not feel like a soul departing or a giving up of a ghost. The ghost already gone, this was the body giving up, responding to my father's ritual it was the symbolic layer departing.

I arrive four minutes before the train is due, grab a tinny from the neighbouring pub, the train enters the station bang on time. I jump on, popping the can. Half an hour later, I am eating a cream tea at Satis House, Yoxford, watching an extended family compose and re-compose themselves for a series of family photographs. Then on to my B&B, Sans Souci, where the landlady's mother tells me that I do not have a room there for tonight, but that her daughter and husband will collect me shortly and drive me to an alternative.

She says there has been a sudden surge of specialist contractors into the area, two thousand of them, for the 'Sizewell Outage', a temporary shutting down and cleaning of the B reactor. A middle-aged man appears and explains that he is not part of the management, but a visitor, a former lodger. He clutches a jar of "the Queen's marmalade". He tells me to visit Bawdsey, where they have an underground radar station and artificial cliffs. "You were in radar, weren't you?" he asks the landlady's mother, who acknowledges the query, but does not elaborate. The military-industrial-domestic complex.

When the landlord and landlady arrive we drive to the alternative B&B, but no one is at home, other than a huge dog, so we visit neighbouring towns for more B&Bs and hotels, including Saxmundham, where there are "troubles" the guest at Lowestoft was escaping from. Without result. The different layers of my hollow doll are gently rattled. Finally, the landlady commandeers the phone at one of the B&Bs and books me into White House Farm, a few miles off at Darsham. I am touched by the time and care spent finding me a room.

White House Farm is a treat. I fetch a liquid supper from a service station. On TV, the second *Transformers* movie; it deploys millions of tons of military hardware in a way that makes the movie's lumbering robots look more tactically appropriate. The Transformers swap around their parts, but that is not transformation.

> *"All places are 'migrant'. And our selves, similarly; not simple, single points of consciousness slipping across neutral planes, but selves that are motion and in motion within and without, extended 'organisms' shaped and shaping relations with each other, reacting to and adapting the geometry of inanimate geographies, cultural transmissions and ideology's reproductive system, moving about basins of attraction, patterned and patterning; a self as likely as any place to be 'just passing through'."*
>
> Phil Smith, 'A Short History of the Future of Walking'

10.10.11

I am confused. Are all the dates in this notebook wrong? Today is Monday, but Monday is not this date. Last night I found myself in a familiar dreamscape; trying to catch a train in a huge railway station where the clocks mutate and the circumstances and reasons for travelling change. I do not remember ever successfully catching a train in one of these dreams. The landlady of the Sans Souci told the landlady here, Mrs Hudson, that I am "on walkabout". Mrs Hudson (I fantasise I am a detective during breakfast)...

Walking in character

DISGUISE IS THE ONLY IDENTITY you need for walking. No further equipment or special clothing is required.

Once walking, there is a mythical-ethical aspect: hold yourself in preparedness for whatever arises. A glove dropped or a toy thrown from a buggy. A stumbling fellow pedestrian. An assault. In Tahrir Square, women created self-protection groups like Tahrir Bodyguard and men formed human shields to protect women protesters from assault. Choose your role. Depending on the character you choose for yourself, and to what layers of mastery of compassion and anger you have ascended, hold yourself always in readiness to accept whatever affordances are given to you.

Any acts of mythic characterisation break down the distance between the doer and their performance, dispersing intellect from actor to action and space, and then from stage directions back to the characters: Pilgrim, Sure Crab, the nomad, the Doctor, Toby the Marxist Tramp, the Small Vicar, Madame Psychogeography, Bell, Goat, Swan, Volkhardt Müller's Company of the Green Man, Comus, Pontiflunk, Signpost, Cecile Oak.

Walk like mist, walk like smoke, walk like muscle, walk like wave, walk like steam.

...tells me about the Sizewell reactor's closing down for cleaning and maintenance: it happens every eighteen months and usually the process lasts six weeks, but this time they have been at it since August in order for extra contractors to have special training for working in cramped conditions. After a good breakfast, I walk fourteen miles non-stop across green concrete, battered by near hurricane winds that sweep across the huge expanses of field;

And those who husbanded the Golden Grain
And those who flung it to the Winds like Rain
Alike to no such aureate Earth are turn'd
As, buried once, Men want dug up again.

Carrying in my head the image of safety-suited contractors working in claustrophobic niches in the reactor, the wind crying in the telephone lines reminds me of the linemen in *It Came From Outer Space*: "there's something in the wires"; monks humming in an electricity sub-station, the fluttering of wind turbines, the lower rumble from giant pylons, the UFO whirr of Sizewell B and the hum that Ivan could hear and I could not. I look in vain for any sign of Thomas Abrams's farm and his ten square yard model of the "Temple of Jerusalem exactly as it was at the beginning of time". The winds have blown it away; picked it up and dissolved it in the full scale. Why not make a full size model of everything? I begin to lose touch with what is around me; walking through winds rather than countryside; one wind blowing through others.

The downside of the liberating hollowing out of the centre is that the wonderful swirling of parts is also the whole thing flying apart.

The day is petering out among The Saints, tiny communities named for a variety of martyrs. Conversation subjects overheard in The Crown Inn, Weybread: 1960s' TV chefs and Benny Hill's impersonation of Fanny Craddock. In between bouts of unconsciousness I am reading the introduction to my copy of Edward FitzGerald's translation of *The Rubaiyat of Omar Khayyam...*

Undercovers

Hold book readings in sheltered, but neglected corners of your town.

...how, while Omar Khayyam might have *written* of wine, what he really *meant* was spirituality. Booze, theatre and death; literary criticism presses them all into dried flowers. Conversation at the Crown moves onto Lady Docker, family genealogy and the aristocracy. The participants speak slowly as if words are to be suffered: "he had the job of opening the pew for Lloyd George", "quadrupled the price... the incomers". I stagger the last few miles to Harleston: today's walking has been an ordeal...

Walking as an ordeal

FOR THE SIDEWAYS WALKING FESTIVAL in Belgium I decided to carry a wooden plinth on my back; an experiment and a burden. I was testing out an idea for our 'ambulant architectures' project in Wrights & Sites. On one of the days we walked 23 miles. I made the mistake of keeping pace with Stephen, who walks a little faster than I do, and the combination of that and the plinth meant that I was exhausted with five miles still to go; foolishly I decided not to stop, but to keep going, while Stephen took over the plinth. I walked the remainder almost in a trance, swinging my arms when I could to keep up momentum. Stephen said I was very bad company; I had no energy to speak. My eyes swelled up and I had difficulty in seeing at times. Yet the experience of the terrain, despite my restricted vision, was revealing and although I collapsed at the destination and had to be immediately helped into a sleeping bag and plied with sweet tea and chocolate (thank you, Amélie, Martin and Simon for looking after me), in the morning I was able to record my experiences:

I am walking in the architecture of a horror film. Each plot, split between brutalism and kitsch is a part of the conspiracy of a grid. Cubes are preyed upon by turrets, turrets by columns. The street is poised to make itself toast cannibal. The dismembered route is memory-less. Suburbia nibbles at blocks of maize – already boxed before it can be harvested. Everywhere but the path is verboden to the walker. Three dogs behind the cage-fence that the people here build around their castles and cubes. Big dog fails to respond to the call of the master. Little dog escapes under the gate and barks at our heels. My eyes swell up at the repetition. "So many people, so little space", everyone says. I see no people. Only the oncoming machine, the concrete channel and at every other plot I hear the different curses of dogs. I see their furious frustrations in the eyes of a capped man, cycling by; he hates our arousal of the grid, he hates me for carrying and not standing on a plinth. My usual walking in the margins, studying detritus like bon mots from Thoreau, botanising the plastic, giggling at signs, not now. I am terrible company; the plinth puts me in the lonely middle of the grid, centre stage of the spectacle. Usually the plinth supports the body, but in this ordeal the body supports the plinth. I am as one piece with the architecture, going blind to see its skeleton, hallucinating in order to hear incantations: property, property, verboden, property, plaster angels, fairies, trolls, wedges of concrete, homes like opened maps, intimate internal diagrams, rendering me a soft speechless white statue carrying its own plinth, the stone in my back turning to yoghurt, bones to salt, gait becoming necessity, a walking zoo made only of ticket office and turnstile, lionless, a population of plaster on an endless canal. I cannot summon the energy to photograph what I came here to see: two neo-classical columns in a neat front lawn. The twin pillars of good and evil, little dog and big dog, interwoven and entangled in the impossible architecture of the final street. They do not reach out to each other, but lurk in their cages, fury chasing frustration in square circles, kitsch dog and brutal dog, maize dog and verboden dog, yap dog and snarl dog walled in their own plots. Amélie, Martin and Simon build an architecture around me: sleeping bag, can of Coke, hot sweet tea.

The man in the mask

HARRY BENSLEY WALKED in an iron masked helmet while pushing a pram; his aim was to walk around the world without being identified. On the pram was a sign: "WALKING ROUND the WORLD". He set off from Trafalgar Square on the first of January in 1908 with a minder he employed. His walk was disrupted in 1914 by the outbreak of world war. He was later a cinema doorman and sat as a Labour Councillor in Wivenoe.

He died in the same month that I was born, May 1956; I wished I had known that when I was pushing my daughter and son in their buggies.

Some stories have him doing all this to win a bet, other versions say it was a punishment to clear a gambling debt.

You don't need a helmet; simply walk around the world without being seen on CCTV or recognised by others. Hide in plain sight. If you wear a hi-viz jacket, to many you will become an invisible labourer with strange powers of access.

...not just the twenty miles against strong winds, but the continuous vulnerability to cars and lorries on pavement-less roads.

The Swan is an old country town hotel; my bedroom looks much as it might have in the 1930s. Who tucks in a duvet? I have a half-timbered bathroom.

The hallucinatory staircase to the bedrooms is out of true, giddy, aspiring to a spiral. The bar, when I arrive, is a cross between a youth club, a building site and an office with all its surfaces covered with invoices. An overwhelming owner emerges from bumf and, with cursory apologies, fails to find a solution to my enquiry about a museum, handing me my key and pointing me in the direction of my room. A mild touch of the Fawlties.

In my room I wash off some of the wet paint picked up in the lobby, and ring the number of the Harleston Museum Curator – I found it in the magazine I thought the owner was fobbing me off with – and she is very helpful. She says that Thomas Abrams's model was on show in Harleston in Bullock Fair Close, but there is now a second-hand bookshop in that building and the model has gone.

I catch the final minutes of the original *Planet of the Apes:* "they did it, the maniacs!" and a BBC programme about the 'Clare Middleton I Love You will u marry me' bridge in Sheffield; often imagined romantically, the BBC turn up a more difficult story. Nick Robinson appears on the BBC News. Watching the local news I am reassured that the elderly man who died in Southwold Harbour was not my experimental rocketeer.

I meet up with Ivan for a drink in The Cherry Tree; this is his home town. He tells me he made a show for the Hush House at Bentwaters; the building has extreme sound-proofing for full-on testing of jet engines inside. The landlord is polishing the bar stools and starts on the shoes of one of the customers: "yes, baas, yes masser!". I feel that I have not been in contact with today, except for a moment to help a lost HGV driver; the process of 'ordeal' was too all encompassing and I need to side-step the physical task a little and find ways to connect with the landscape of isolated farms, 'footprint' moments for virtual families and agricultural outsourcing. I am due to walk there again tomorrow.

11.10.11

I dreamed of visiting heritage tourism sites that were like funfair rides, the visitors flung about and whirled around. I have some sort of virus, a chest infection – nothing too severe, but a sore throat, cough, and so on. Above the breakfast cereal and fruit juice table, the wall is decorated with bomb fragments.

After breakfast I leave The Swan Hotel and go knocking at the door of the charity bookshop in Bullock Fair Close behind the hotel. There is a light on at the back of the shop. After knocking twice, the door is answered by a woman. Her teeth seem to have lives quite independent of each other. She is very helpful and explains that the model of the Temple at Jerusalem was displayed here up until ten years ago, when it was taken to Needham and put on show there; though it is not presently on display. She describes the impact that seeing the model had on her, emphasising the magnitude of the impression it made, though she is unable to give me a material detail that might make it vivid for me. Thomas Abrams died a year ago.

Now wandering the farm land beyond Harleston, I am beginning to wonder if this is a non-mythogeographical or even anti-mythogeographical territory. I seem to be at war with it. Yes, of course, each cabbage in each cabbage field is different. Each of the few people I meet has a unique life. But there has been homogenising here, large-scale industrialised agriculture on a predominantly flat landscape. There are very few hedges, very few insects, nothing of the multiplicity of detail from which to easily construct a weave; yet it would still be easy to mistake it for countryside. Terry Aldous's pamphlet-length childhood autobiography, *Growing up in The Saints in the 1940s and 1950s*, describes a secular and industrialised working life: paraffin lamps, telly, "Vimto and a packet of crisps". But what there also is here is a plane, a reminder of how what is striated and controlled runs through every feature of itself, not externally controlled but patterned from within its own texture and grain. Authority is unusually exposed out here; it runs through everything, right to the surfaces, a vivid anonymity, moving to the beat of a spectacular humdrum that until now I could not hear.

The Otter Trust is unsigned and forbidding. Plain angular Methodist chapels reinforce the anaesthetic ambience. The fear of 'the dog in general' is real and particular to me here; I brace myself as I approach each isolated farm or house gate. Seeing no dogs, my fear of the general shapeless dogfear is all the greater.

An immense military transporter plane in battlefield green livery rises from below some trees and disappears behind a rise in the next field. In the distance I can see vintage aircraft, collected and bloodless. I have carried my Grandad's medal with me, the size of an exit wound, but where is the theatre of blood? I have been through the dead zones of the Cold War, but we are the butchers, the snipers, the Slaughterhouse Smiths, loaders, rootless guns for hire, agents and spectres working in holey space; where is our abattoir?

The names of trails – The Godric Way, The Boudicca Way – seem even more bogus than usual. This is a melancholy road; I am not concerned that it will immobilise me now, but that it itself is beginning to silt up and grind towards a halt.

It comes as a relief, at first, to enter Bungay; a large red sign heralding it as "a fine old town". But my general fear has colonised the town; everywhere is the Black Dog; on gate posts and doorsteps, in the names of societies and retail outlets. A concept in variable shapes; a noticeboard tells me that it came "in the midst of fire"; the great walk is working.

The entrance to the castle ruins is through Jesters Café, where I eat some afternoon tea sat opposite a historical display and a lavatory that are presented identically. In the display is a photograph of a pageant in the ruins; a horse covered entirely in a white cloth but for eyeholes reminds me of the white deer on the edge of the forest. Elizabeth Bonhôte, a gothic novelist, bought the castle ruins in the eighteenth century and had a house built between its twin towers. There she wrote her gothic novel *Bungay Castle*, published in 1796. Her earlier novel, of 1772, *The Rambles of Mr Frankly*, inspired by Sterne's *A Sentimental Journey*, in turn inspired its own sub-genre of rambler fictions...

Women and walking

THIS IS THE BIG ONE around walking – so obvious and banal.

And out of it and around it and if we grasp the centrality of it, then everything else can come from it.

The question of women and their relation to public space – to the streets and squares, to the public spaces of power – sacred spaces, protest spaces, educational spaces, working spaces, dance floor spaces, political spaces – and their rights of access and agency in the overlapping spaces of public and private life, public and relationship space, personal and family space.... without a politics of the walking of these, there is no hope at all in walking.

I live in one of the safest and, in some ways, most liberal places to live in the world, and yet I teach women students who are shocked by the idea that they might make a destination-less wander around this city; they rush from a to b as quickly as they can, avoiding eye contact, avoiding any contact... of course, there is no such thing as riskless, but the narrative of risk that they have found themselves in is radically limiting their lives. They fear the world here, they fear others here. When however, they do take up an offer to walk, they are often amazed by how generous much of the world is, both the affordances of its physical masses and textures and the everyday indifference or friendliness of its passers-by.

There is nothing 'irrational' about these fears; the reality of the threats and the reality of the fears they generate are parts of the same oppression.

I sometimes read or hear a familiar refrain: that any woman walking on the streets is (and historically has always been) automatically taken for a 'streetwalker', a prostitute. Coming from a working-class family living in an industrial Midlands city, I know that for much of their working lives my mother and her mother walked to work in factories and offices in the morning and out to the pictures or dances in the evening, along with tens of thousands of other women in the city. The common assumption was not that these women were prostitutes; on the other hand some men, and in some cultures this may extend to most men, like to entertain the fantasy that any independent woman in a public space is automatically sexually available to them.

In many parts of the world women are grossly restricted by habitual, officially, theocratically and politically ignored or condoned, and very immediate threats of violence. As I write, almost a hundred women protesting in Cairo's Tahrir Square have been subject to sexual assault on one day alone. But the cause of women struggling with and against violence in public space is not aided by the restriction of other women by exaggerated narratives of threat that reproduce a twisted male fantasy about their public sexual availability.

I once saw this played out at a conference session on walking. A male delegate stood up and bemoaned the male bias in psychogeographical walking, complaining that women were barely ever present on psychogeographical drifts. It had to be pointed out to him that the entire speaking panel was made up of psychogeographically-inclined female walkers. So, in like manner, for anyone who thinks that women don't (let alone shouldn't) walk or that women are absent from the ranks of dérivistes and artist-walkers:

Peace Pilgrim (Mildred Norman) walked 25,000 miles for peace, Kinga Araya created a walk for the route of the former Berlin Wall, Julia Solis is an urban explorer, Alison Lloyd combines mountain walking and contemporary art, Janet Cardiff makes audio walks, Ana Laura Lopez de la Torre engages with political walking, Morag Rose founded the Loiterers Resistance Movement, Sophie Calle stalked, Elspeth Owen makes epic yet intimate walks delivering messages, Sophia New maps with Dan Belasco Rogers as plan b, Emma Bush created a performance walk around her village, Caroline Saunders walked a wolf onto a forest, Barbara Lounder makes art with the prosthetics of walking, Kerrie Reading swanned around Erdington, Karine Maussière makes urban promenades, Gail Burton crawled in 'Aisle (for GHost III)' with Marc Vaulbert de Chantilly and makes walking events with Clare Qualmann and Serena Korda as walkwalkwalk, Jo Daccombe and LJ Klée made a Dream Walking night tour, Esther Pilkington walked the route of Richard Long's 'Crossing Stones' (1987) and then created a performance: 'a long walk', Louise Ann Wilson creates mobile performances across wild landscapes, Helen Drever made meditational walks, Claudia Zeiske is a driving force in Deveron Arts' walking projects, Ruth Ben-Tovin worked with people in Peterborough to create their own guided tours, live artist Dot Howard performed a 'backstage tour', Agnieszka Kozlowska conducted walking projects for three years, Jess Allen walked between wind farms for her 'Tilting At Windmills', Antonia Beck makes audio walks, Jennie Savage has used the audio guide and the guided walk in her artwork, Claire Blundell Jones walked with a tumbleweed, Jen Southern made a walk for virtual accompaniment, Monali Meher created a silent walk, Hannah Sullivan drifted in Bristol (UK) simultaneously with walkers in Bristol (Rhode Island, USA) for '34 Bristols', The Miss Guides of Vancouver perform tours of their city, Emma Cocker is a theorist of space and walking, Gemma Seltzer walked the banks of the Thames for 'Look Up At The Sky', Sarah Bowen makes stop-frame movies on epic walks, my

15-year-old daughter Rachel woke me at 6.30am during the writing of this book to say she was going off walking with her friend, Lottie Child makes games for the streets, Nic Green walked from her home to the sea and back, Ellie Harrison is planning a soundwalk for her Grief Series, Kira O'Reilly encouraged walkers to flock silently, Maryclare Foa driftsings, Marlene Creates makes walks of site-specific poetry, Ana Teresa Fernandez stood in a gutter in stilettos of ice until they melted, Yael Sherill curated a festival of innovative tours in Berlin, Sara Wookey choreographs everyday urban walking in 'unwalkable' US cities, Ania Bas set up the Walking Reading Group, Misha Myers created a city wall walk with line dancers and leads the Walking Library with Dee Heddon who is walking 40 different walks with 40 friends for her 40th birthday, Carol Robertson and Michèle Roberts created a book of paintings and writings generated from their solo walks, Laura Nanni and Sorrel Muggridge made a walkwork spanning 3978km with a piece of rope, Anoushka Athique made walks for 'Mobile Machinoeki' and 'The Fabulous Walks' and recently a fabric walk, Marie-Anne Lerjen creates walks for architectural exploration, Tina Richardson (Madame Psychogeography) is a schizocartographical psychogeographer, Simone Kenyon and Tamara Ashley created a walk-dance along the length of The Pennine Way, Anna Francis led tours of a former National Garden Festival site, Laurie Anderson made 'Walk' for World Expo 05, Charlotte Frost makes anti-capitalist movies on foot, Jodi Patterson marks the routes of her drifts, Vanessa Grasse makes choreographic audio walks, Monique Besten walks in a suit into which she stitches images and poems and she walked naked, Katie Etheridge's 'Field Work' took walkers in search of Brighton's mediaeval field system, Cathy Turner of Wrights & Sites creates provocative guides and manifestos for ambulant explorers and architect-walkers, Amy Cutler was arrested for walking like a zombie, Sozita Goudouna turned garage doors into pages for a reading walk, Natalie Doonan (Curator of Love) has been mapping and matching people's routes through their

city, Eddie Ladd learned how to 'walk like a man', Donna Shilling walked back to her college on its closing, Jane Samuels walks abandoned buildings and makes art there, Heather McCann and Kristin Parker were members of Boston's 'People's Tours', Walking With Our Sisters in Canada protests the missing, Lonnie van Brummelen dragged Hermes from Amsterdam to Lascaux, Nicola Singh organised a parade to explore architectural space through movement, Lucy Frears makes ambulant audioworks, Beatrice Jarvis uses dance to find places of reflection in the forest (including the jungle of the cities), Ali Pretty leads walks with installations to the white horses of Wiltshire, Hilary Ramsden and Erika Block mapped and made performances for desire paths, Jooyoung Lee led 'Let's walk and chat together', Siân Lacey Taylder is a ramblanista, Yvonne Lake creates psychogeographic city tours, Anna Townley walked between a city's morgue and its crematorium with Lawrence Bradby, Susanne Kudielka works with Kaspar Wimberley to organise Stuttgart Arttours, Sandra Reeve made a performance journey on a footpath, the Daring Girl Gang prowl alleys, parks and graveyards at night, Amy Sharrocks made a phone walk, Alison Knowles made a Franco-American Tour with Robert Filliou, Rachel Gomme knitted as she walked a line of yarn, Sue Palmer led a walk around the "unexamined corners" of Portland with Joff Winterhart, Germander Speedwell walks waywardly the symbols of London... and on and on...

Now, please, don't tell me that there are no women walking...

Writing this section I have been indebted to the work of Dee Heddon and Cathy Turner who have worked to open the eyes of the academy to women's walking. In their recent essay 'Walking Women: Shifting the Tales and Scales of Mobility' they describe how the gendered valuing of "individualist, heroic, epic and transgressive" walking works to exclude more relational and convivial walking and marginalise those women whose walking does not fit these privileged, and predominantly male-dominated, tags. (But even they repeat the old canard: "[t]he historical and contemporary landscapes of psychogeographical practices are mostly devoid of women"; tell that to Tina Richardson or Morag Rose... I think it may be time to make a very clear distinction between what the dominant narratives and values tell us that walking women do and what those women, in the face of both real physical challenges and tales of their absence, actually do.) While acknowledging that some women do walk heroically, individualistically and trangressively and thereby are sometimes allowed to slip into the realm of what is valued in walking, Dee and Cathy, without recourse to a feminine essentialism, point to some key qualities in the work and art of many women walkers that, despite constraints to keep them "local", despite codings of female bodies that attract unwelcome and unwelcomed attention, despite complicity "in maintaining the monumental" and a critical discourse that renders the female walker absent, continue to challenge divisive, binary scales of the epic and intimate in walking and mobilise the political potential of walking to create new social relationships rather than produce extreme repetitions of the same old ambulating.

Cathy and Dee's essay not only contains crucial arguments and accounts, but is itself a model for something that is happening; as it swings slowly from a critique of reactionary and exclusive discourses around walking to the actual practices of increasing numbers of women making aesthetic and activist walking in public space.

At the same time, it isn't rosy-tinted-spectacles time yet. It is not simply the presence (or threat) of violence on the streets that is the problem here, but it is exacerbated where the survivors of that violence (actual or threatened) are made absent; an absence that rots and erodes the public space, a void that fills up with propagandising fear, an emptiness that speaks by word of mouth, by fictions and fables mixing with honest reports of suffering, a nothingness on legs that moves among the playgrounds and at the school gates and between the friendships and across the families, handing out invisible maps of where young women, all women, cannot go. So the Free World is not free, the liberal world is not liberal, and every right of way is halved; public places made pubic places. It is crucial that women get out of their houses; that's where the murders and the assaults mostly take place. The community that is gated against a fear of what is outside is also a convenient imprisoning of half of those within it. A new negotiation of global public space is necessary – not a puritanisation, but one by which an exchange of numerous energies is possible without violence. Otherwise, we are allowing the rapist and the psychopath to run our streets if we cannot be friendly or flirtatious with each other.

Just as people run (and should run, if they are brave enough) towards the victims of bombings, to distressed strangers they do not know, so we need to address the rights of the stranger on the street; to allow meaningless encounters and trivial situations to multiply, to allow a lack of significance back into the everyday and to wrestle meaningless and trivial space from those who would flood it with theological, cultural and familial restrictions and mono-meanings, to make it free for all those groups who might suffer – or fear they might suffer – assault, violation or intimidation on the road.

Walking needs to put its own house in order, identifying those gross prejudices that it has inherited from its romantic traditions: "women.... are too personal for the high enjoyment of going a journey. They will be forever thinking about you or about themselves... They cannot rise to that philosophic plane of mind that is the very marrow of going a journey... You are in their society, they are in yours; and the multitudinous personal ties which connect you all to.... society" (Robert Cortes Holliday) – which, despite itself, makes a good argument for the opposite point of view: that there's no better reason for walking than sociableness and a multiplicity of connections.

Until all women are free to walk wherever they choose and without fear, any so-called "high enjoyment of going a journey" will continue to be a reactionary illusion, a fluid prison in which some are more stuck than others.

"No march, movement, or agenda that defines manhood in the narrowest terms and seeks to make women lesser partners in this quest for equality can be considered a positive step."   Angela Davis

...I am rather sad that the house within Bungay Castle has gone; but the dark formless shape between the towers, a black gothic décolletage, is impressive. I wander the ruins; aimless and detached; I drift the streets of the town, walking them as if they were ruined too. The statue of Justice here is not blindfolded; hubristic, she must deliver judgement without the benefit of randomness.

On Bridge Street, without knowing what I am looking for, I find an old abattoir; still with its bullock hoist in place, huge rusted butchery tools, long thin spades and hooks like giant fish barbs, hanging over double doors; maybe this is something like the one my great-grandfather ran in nearby Halesworth. Earlier in the day, on the edge of Harleston, I had passed BONES APART PET PRODUCTS. Then a roadside shrine to an accident victim. On this walk Death has not melted into the Mist of melancholy. Today I was upset by how many smashed animals I encountered. Not the dry, flattened travesties of previous days, but piles of bleeding intestines and brains: rats, rabbits, snakes, pheasants, squirrels, hedgehogs. Death is not a mist, not a plane, but a dirty weave of bits, a broken thing requiring more and more broken things to make its gothic swirls. It is nothing in itself, and it is this nothing that is awful. That is the only difficult and inevitable thing about Mum's death: Mum is not here any more. I want Mum to be here, but time does not grant my wishes. Bear the loss, crack your shoulders and start remembering Mum's life, not just her death. I cannot do this yet. This, among many other things, is where I have not succeeded in re-enacting Sebald's trajectory...

Re:enactment

RECREATE IN LOCAL, accessible forms some of the 'classic' walks:

- Sophie Calle's 'Suite Vénitienne' or Vito Acconci's 'Following Piece' – subtle stalking pieces
- Peter Bodenham and Simon Whitehead's '2mph'; taking a stuffed goose on a drovers' route from Aberteifi in Wales to Smithfield Market in London.
- Claire Blundell Jones's 'Tumbleweed' in which she blows a tumbleweed through public spaces using an industrial leaf blower.
- Marina Abramović and Ulay walking the Great Wall of China towards each other to meet and mark the ending of their relationship.

You might evolve and learn a 'medley' of mini-versions of such walks, a sort of "history of extraordinary walking" to be re-walked for a few minutes at a moment's notice.

...I am with him on the depressive interweaving, but, I break down my sources more; the danger is that it is to nothingness and meaningless that I break them down. But a mythogeographer's obligation is to dismantle properties, and the better I get at it, the less I admire myself. This is the principle of hypocrisy; if the ideas and tactics I stumble across on these journeys are to have any use, then they have to work for hypocrites like me.

Dismantling myself a little further, I have begun to aimlessly wander about the side streets; places as broken up as I am. The shops are filled with Halloween costumes; a large paper skeleton leans on the bottle racks of a wine shop. On the window of a betting shop, in a composite illustration of football, horse and greyhound, the dog is black and sulphurous.

Opposite these bookmakers I find the old abattoir; set back a little from the road; watchful; something peeping from a shell. I raise my camera but I am stopped by an elderly man who materialises from the neighbouring pub. He angrily marches into shot and begins to erect a green Brechtian half-curtain across the path up to the abattoir. He says nothing, but seems highly disturbed by my presence. I do not feel I can speak to him. He is protecting something or hiding something; something that he imagines or something he imagines that I imagine. I pretend to be interested in the large windowed property next door to the abattoir; behind its

dusty windows is an expanse of barely ordered and grimy bric-à-brac. Despite the multiplicity of objects – painted eggs, tin soldiers, banknotes, a wailing china doll, Union Jack Corn Paste, Brasso – their juxtapositions mean nothing to me, though there might be a map of my whole walk here. The parts are immobile. I am facing it now; there's nothing wrong with me, it's not my psyche breaking down, but it is the mythogeography that has become stuck, twitching like an old VHS player on pause. The more I explore the filthy window display the more nightmarish is its leering back: sentimental shepherdesses, transparent Toby Jugs, a racist engraving called 'Fleecing The Lamb'. Parts without a motor; I can make neither sense nor place of it. It does not like the way I have used it as a decoy; stepping to the side of itself, into the wings, it is to one side of its own existence, unreachable. The whole damned thing is here laid out for me in symbols and I have approached it wrongly, deceitfully, inauthentically, and it has skittered away like three brown hares across a minefield.

I peer around the corner of the building, but the guardian has not been fooled and stands his ground, glaring. I walk quickly away, disheartened and unnerved. In a High Street window a glass-topped table supported by sculptures of two bent black slave women bears a large SOLD notice.

Ivan told me last night of a meeting with one of the radical playwright Arnold Wesker's descendants; later he had read in a local newspaper of this individual's heading a campaign against locally encamped travellers.

Sometimes I smell like I'm rotting away. Bits of me are more alive than ever before and bits of me have almost passed away. Variegation. Life-death. The gargoyle on the North Wall of St Mary's looks very like a dog...

Urfaces

ALL AROUND US ARE ACCIDENTAL GARGOYLES or 'throats', heads engraved unthinkingly into the surface of the landscape that are then connected to hidden bodies of knowledge and desire everywhere...

We walk among a far denser population than we know.

Just as in the Templar Knights' graffiti in their gatehouse prison at Domme, where the gaps between the prisoners' scratched symbols and their satirical sketches are filled with thousands and thousands of tiny faces, so we, prisoners of a single body, are kept company by faces all around us emerging from the Multiplicities beneath the Samsāra.

...outside the West Door of St Mary's I am tempted by the "druid's stone" which, according to a notice, children believe can be used to summon the Devil by walking around it twelve times; then a voice comes from *inside* the stone. I want to do it. I should do it. The notice is a performance text, a script, and it is my theatrical obligation to act it out. To hear the voice *inside* stone; perhaps to speak in stone. Maybe that is what I have been trying to do; in all these churches and priories and castle ruins and pebble beaches and shingle streets and across grinded sands; preparing to speak in stone. I am too scared; but I know I am going to have to speak stone sometime soon.

Scatty with disappointment and fear, I sneak back to the abattoir, but the green half-curtain is still in place and after taking one quick shot I run away.

Back at my B&B, I hide for a while; Billy Connolly is on TV waxing lyrical about a car called *The Pimp*. Lottery winners, models. "Find the Poker Star in you." I switch off. I sit in the living room, looking out of the window across the Flatland I walked earlier, a triangle advancing base first, at a striated sunset orange and red. I am reading about the town's Black Dog in Dr. David Waldron and Christopher Reeve's excellent *Shock! The Black Dog of Bungay*. Pat, my landlady, has gone to a private view at the Black Dog Society; a club for local artists.

Shock! offers a close analysis; it *locates* its story. Local records recount a lightning strike on St Mary's Church during a remarkably vicious storm in 1577, killing two people sheltering there. The first record of a black dog racing down the aisle and burning members of the congregation, however, comes later, in a pamphlet published about the event by a London writer, a puritan by the name of Fleming. He does not seem to have ever visited the town. He places the fatalities in the nave of St Mary's, though the local records put the deaths in the belfry. It is possible that there was local collusion with Fleming, from the neighbouring, and rival, low and more Protestant church of Holy Trinity. There had been a long-running religious dispute between the two congregations and, perhaps even worse, a dispute about the removal of a rood screen *within* the congregation of St Mary's itself just prior to the storm.

Fleming extends his exotic narrative a few miles to Blythburgh, where the black dog leaps up on the 'idolatrous' rood screen there. The message is clear: Popish sin has brought on the devil-dog's attack.

This sectarian tale was occasionally but decreasingly referenced over subsequent centuries as Bungay's culture became increasingly industrialised, the town becoming known as 'Little London', until the 1930s when the silting up of the river and a wider Depression undermined the industries here. The local Reeve of the time, a Dr Cane, set out to reinvigorate the town's historical self-consciousness with excavations at the Castle, and revived the story of the Black Dog, reconstructing the town's history and inventing new rituals. Dr Cane's material improvements included replacing a damaged Town Pump with an electric lamp light decorated with an image of the Dog; a competition among local children to choose its design cannily suppressed criticism.

There was a wiping clean of the slate: shed, chicken coops and allotments around the castle ruins were destroyed. Just as the original tale responded to deep divisions in the 1570s around ritual, reformation and the subsequent zig zags of royal religious policy, so in the 1930s the revival of the Black Dog of Bungay fitted with a general privileging of rural authenticity, a refocusing on an idealised pre-modern past after the disappointment of industrialism. Dr Crane post-modernises the town as a 'destination' under a black flag of demonology dressed up as cute 'folklore'; replacing industry with a desirable image.

There was nothing opportunistic about Crane's fabrication. It was fully authentic, loyal to the shape's original flexibility, appearing first as a "horribly shaped thing" before taking on a canine semblance. To me it is simply the shadow of my fear; the scratching of claws on the concrete yard of a farm or across the tarmac of a pavement, it is the shapeless thing that churns my anxieties for what lies ahead, it is the scratching that is always at my back, the past that will finally hunt me down, the ghost that ends my journey and pins me to the road. There is no escaping its brand here. I keep myself temperate by enjoying the thought of another town with the same story where they have adopted an unidentifiable, amoebic, "horribly shaped thing" as their brand image.

The late Theo Brown, a folklorist whose works I am a little familiar with, working much in my home city and county, proposed that spectral black dogs in general were "a projection of the Shadow, the repository of the dark anxieties, desires and drives of the unconscious mind". Yep. It falls into place. In the midst of fire, the white deer, the black dog, all in the crucible of the walk; the working is becoming more transparent, but it is unfinished.

I abandon my idea of visiting Ditchingham. Despite the appeal of finding Haggard's Norfolk pyramids and volcanoes, I know there is no resolution for me there; there has been enough fire. Now has come the moment to abandon the Sebald route. It has led me as far as it can. The road has melted and inundated the whole terrain. I must do the next part of the work alone; but not immobilised.

My reparative catatonia, at fourteen, was defensive, but now my fabricated selves are Aggressors; tactical, positive, layered and charmed. Tomorrow I must catch the 588 bus to Halesworth at 9.40am from Trinity Street, at the stop between Holy Trinity Church and St Mary's. Albedo, nigredo, solar fire – there can only be a resolution of these in rubedo. Blood.

12.10.11

This morning I am drawn back to the giant lozenge-shaped 'druid's stone'. Its angle, at variance with the gravestones standing to attention, means something. I slightly fear it. Its proportions suggest that much of it has sunken beneath the surface over the millennia. I consider for the umpteenth time walking the twelve times around the stone and asking it a question. There is no way that I will. When stones speak is when coasts crumble. Monsters are warnings. In Chesterton's *The Man Who Was Thursday*, a table in a down-at-heel beerhouse that serves lobster mayonnaise turns like a screw, detaches itself and plunges downwards, reaching a deep red-lit room with a door that leads to a spherical room full of spherical bombs. Before the Zeppelin came down in Suffolk the locals saw a red light in the sky. Cyclops eye. The world is full of tunnels. And mine shafts. And bunkers. But I am not ready, yet, to be a stone's philosopher. Death is far less scary than such a change.

I wander around the graves in St Mary's churchyard; the urns and skulls on the stones, a row of coffin-shaped tombs. Over a doorway some martyr is being pinned to the road by a sharp clawed beast. On another a formless shape. The only marriage I can make out here is Death to Heritage; spawning the phantom pregnancy prematurely christened Timeless Identity. But what if the affair were to be reversed? Then continuity would rest only in non-continuity; we would be preserved only in fire; happy only when we accept that our children will choose differently from us and nothing will repeat. Over and over and over and over again.

Such a morbid temporality wires up these crumbling funerary symbols in the damp churchyard to the compulsive accumulations of mythogeography's 'and and and', chiming disturbingly with a frictionless novelty once described by Guy Debord as "paralyzed memory". Yet, I sense, in the graveyard, an affordance, inside the monumental obliteration. That Thomas Browne's "timeless present", encrypted within the Sebaldian prose that keeps looping around in my head, constitutes a parthenogenetic checkmating of itself, a shadow not of annihilation but of the revelation of a combined and uneven apocalypse. Not an eternal present then, but a future's present; a way of taking pleasure again and again in the future (enjoying all the crumblings to come!) while passing on that pleasure now (through this description, for example). In other words, by reversing deferred gratification, and by deferring the obliteration bit of apocalypse while hanging on to its illuminating thrills, we can abolish an addictive present that forever negates what it has in deference to its need to have it again and again. Now, isn't that a timeline for an 'ecstatic' heritage in which we might finally acknowledge what all those memorials, bequests, titles, tombs and monuments have been desperately signalling to us for so long: their utter horror at our attempts to preserve them, their longing for us to let them rest gently into the arms and arts of decomposition and fire, not prop them up like mummies in costumes?

I catch the bus. It runs on time. Anxious not to miss it, I was up at 7.26am. On the TV News, the US is accusing the Revolutionary Guard in Iran of plotting an assassination on American soil. It feels like the Cold War again today. Next story up: the UK's retreating shore line. On the bus I retrieve from the bottom of my rucksack a map of Halesworth given to me by my Dad; in pencil he has written the names of two roads given to him by the local museum when he passed this way a few years back, possible locations the museum staff believed that the Smiths had butcher's shops.

I visit the library and then the local history museum at the station. I pore over the directories for hour after hour. Unfortunately, being a Smith complicates genealogy. *White's 1844 Suffolk Directory* – there is a William Smith in Pound Street (a bailiff) and in Church Lane – Henry, Robert and John Smith, carriers. In 1875

(*Kelly's Suffolk Directory*) there is a John Smith (private resident) in Pound Street, and a Samuel Smith & Co. – carriage builders – in Bridge Street and a Charles Duncan Smith on the London Road (a farmer). No butchers called Smith listed under 'Commercial' in *Kelly's 1900 Suffolk Directory*. George Smith, pork butcher and painter, London Road, in 1844; there is a George Smith in Mill Hill Street who was a Painter, Plumber or Glazier, in 1875 there's a James Smith, carpenter & builder in "Mill Hill". *1830 – Pigot & Co. Directory*: George Smith, under Painters, Plumbers & Glaziers. *1839 – Pigot & Co. Directory*: George Smith, under painters, etc., in Mill Street. *Robson Directory* of 1839 has a George Smith as Plumber & Glazier, and Henry, Robert and John Smith as carriers. 1851 Census – George Smith (Glazier) is down as being in Thoroughfare (Bridge Street is not listed separately, so it may mean Bridge Street), aged 46, born in Halesworth, property now on Camelot Yard as described in 1979, ten properties away from the bridge on the western side of Thoroughfare. 1855, Robert Smith was a policeman, living in Bridge Street. 1858, *Suffolk Directory*, Robert and John Smith are listed as brickmakers and farmers, Church Farm. Samuel Smith is a coach builder in Bridge Street (also in 1864). Mr John Smith, Pound Street, 1873. In 1874 there is a Mrs Sarah Smith (& Co.) in Bridge Street and a Thomas Smith, builder & joiner, in Mill Street. 1879: Henry Smith, pork butcher, Bridge Street. By 1883 he has moved, he is now a pork butcher in Quay Street (also there in *1885, Suffolk Directory*). In 1892 no reference to any Smith being a butcher. 1896, George Smith is a pork butcher in Pound Street. 1900, George Smith (butcher & painter), Pound Street. 1903, 83 London Road, (George Smith). *Gales Almanac, 1904*, still at 83 London Road (and 1906 and 1908 also). There's also a Mrs Smith at 23 Quay Street – could this be Henry's former shop in Quay Street? It may be the former coachbuilders from Bridge Street? 1904: no mention of Smiths as butchers. 1913: Harry Smith, 7 Swan Lane; is that Grandad (Harry Barnard Smith)? From 1903 there is an Arthur Edward Smith listed at 3 Bridge Street, but no profession given. In 1916 there is now a William Herbert Smith at 7 Swan Lane (brother took over from Grandad while he was in France?) In 1925 a William Herbert Smith at 3 Station Road. I walk to 83 London Road (formerly Pound Street) and 7 Swan Lane, I look at the outsides of the properties, I knock on both doors; no one is at home at either. Am I looking at anything? 7 Swan Lane has a For Sale sign and I collect the details from the estate agents, but I am not looking at *anything*. Given erosion, changes, context, redecoration, replacement, light, renovation, burning, cleaning, gaze – what is there left? No one is at home. I begin to work my way along Bridge Street and Thoroughfare, looking for clues, asking in shops about former uses. I call at the present-day butcher's by the bridge on Thoroughfare (formerly Bridge Street) where the owner, Mr Palmer, suggests that a shop opposite, on the far side of the stream, might be one of the places I am looking for. I prevaricate before ringing the bell.

The shop owner, young and boyish, dressed smart casual, neat thin hair, answers and after my halting explanation invites me inside. He says that he too has heard that the shop was once a butcher's and more recently a cobbler's and a chippie.

There is no evidence that I can see of cobbler's or chippie or butcher's; the owner says that I am welcome to check out the cellar below if I think I might find something there. What ensues is for me one of the highlights of my walking...

A few highlights from other drifts and wanders (3)

ᵀH Stepping onto Brunel's Tamar Bridge, 120 feet above the river, with Paul, a fellow vertigo sufferer, who up till then had only ever crossed the bridge (and many, many times across four decades) by car or bus, never before on foot. Completing the ordeal together we walked into Plymouth searching out the tops of buildings...

ᵀH In Belgium we came across a set of Christian shrines, one for each of the Stations of the Cross, the Via Dolorosa, markers on Christ's journey to Golgotha and resurrection. Arriving from the wrong direction we walked them backwards: Jesus fell from heaven, plunging through a tomb and was impaled on a cross, onlookers sucked tears back into their eyes, the cross was lowered and the nails extracted from his body and he was dressed. Jesus walked backwards, falling and rising, his cross like a giant rubber erasing his route, Veronica smeared his face with grime and sweat, while Simon of Cyrene took and then handed him back his cross. Jesus left his mother and arrived at the court of the Sanhedrin where he was forgiven and freed.

ᵀH Walking alone along an old canal ignoring the signs saying the path was closed up ahead, I 'sailed through' as if I could walk through walls.

ᵀH Walking for hours in Devon woods with Sandra, Cathy and Simon, unsure of our direction, suddenly the trees opened up on a massive grass auditorium and there was our city, preening itself in the afternoon sun.

ᴴ Looking up on a city centre drift with the artists of Blind Ditch to see what I can only describe as a bird on fire in the night sky (I still have no explanation).

ᴴ With fifty others on Berry Head dancing the collision of Gondwana and Laurasia.

ᴴ Being thrown out of a London trinkets shop with such doyen/ne/s of walking as Jim Colquhoun, Maryclare Foa, Rev. John Davies and David Pinder.

ᴴ With Simon, scouting for a route for a Witches 400 walk in the fields around Newchurch-in-Pendle, we met only one other person; she turned out to be a Nutter, a descent of Alice Nutter, one of the women whose judicial murder 400 years previously we were commemorating.

...I make my way warily down the narrow stone steps, raw bricks graze a shoulder, there is a single naked light bulb below, appropriate for a place of id, I am Lila Crane in the fruit cellar, and it briefly occurs to me that I have cornered myself. The shopkeeper stands at the top of the stairs, I note how unexpectedly cool it is, I check just to make sure that he does not actually keep a b... o, he does, in one of the recesses, surrounded by piles of human clutter, a bike, piles of board games, large plastic bags of Brazier coke, frazzled leather suitcases, carpets, a vacuum cleaner and numerous dirty plastic containers, sits a human skull, a desultory jawless ornament. There to underline the metaphorical point, that whatever happens here is somehow existential, subjective, non-linguistic; the clue, then, is in what is absent. But, what? How do I deduce... for all the jumble, I cannot even see the room, only slowly does it emerge from the starkness of the light and the severe reflections from glossy packaging and white plastic; the older frame of what was here; whitewashed rough plaster, an arch of bricks above a fireplace, a sink beside which are long ridges in the wall as if a shelf or work surface was once fixed there. And underfoot, tiles, reddish brown, smooth, cambered, ceramic, clayish, their surfaces mottled and chipped, stained mostly with smears of a spilled white substance, but then flecks of something deep red in the cracks and dents, some of this is red and powdery like old paint, some of it like something else, something darker, thicker.

From the top of the stairs the shopkeeper is saying something about a former girlfriend, and the river being full of bones, bones from an abattoir. I turn and turn and turn trying to put together the different parts of the cellar, woozily calibrating the work surfaces and sinks, fireplaces and recesses; the parts are not fitting and I stumble. The cellar has a sloping floor; the cellar sinks down towards one corner, where in the white painted bricks is a drain.

The shopkeeper joins me now, as I speak what I see and we are together making guesses, deductions, we are manufacturing heritage, self-consciously adding, accumulating, telling, conjuring images. A meat preparation surface, nails to hang the knives, the sink to wash the meat, the coolness of the cellar to preserve it, the sloping floor and the run off through a drain to the river, the river full of bones... I point my camera at the skull and the owner says: "my girlfriend's expecting in a few weeks – hence all the clutter".

This is not a room. The blood is not in the river, the blood is here, on the floor of the cellar, dried in the dents, this is a room of meat and blood, four years of killing, we are up to our ankles in offal, I don't know what I set out to find, but it is here, the change of quantity that changes quality, the place and time when numbers turn into a human being, a few scraps of story into a myth, a middle-aged baby drenched in rubedo.

Grandad, heritage, melancholy. All here, purified, decomposed, burnt, and now spilling, ankle deep. And I have no farther to go. And I have no mother to go to.

Only as I climb the stairs does it strike me, rising, orphaned, from the immersion of the cellar bowl, flooded with rubedo, that there might be some significance in my ascending into a goldsmith's.

I walk about the town for a while, dazed, trying, half-heartedly to get some sense of the shapes through which Grandad passed as a child and in young adulthood: police station, Rifle Hall, courthouse.

And the metaphorical animals on the Ancient House in the Thoroughfare – did he puzzle over them? Images of Saxon warriors on buildings, did they help form his ideas about joining an army? Non-conformist chapels, a churchyard, its gravestones already 150 years old when Grandad was here, all through the town our family's buildings filled with animal blood, its waters full of bones.

I do feel melancholy now; I am homesick now, I feel no private or personal identity here; even the slight pressure to feel something, and the sure knowledge that there is nothing to be found except the looking itself, is weighing on me. Feeling weakened by the virus too; sore throat, raw drain. I sit on a wall near the station and try to change my train ticket for an early service with a woman in a call centre far away, but there is no flexibility...

> 'There's no difference', the schoolmaster said, 'between peasants and castle.' Maybe', said K., 'but that doesn't alter my situation. Might I come and see you some time?' 'I live in Swan Lane, at the butcher's.'"
>
> Franz Kafka, The Castle

..as in my travel dreams, I never set off, I cannot find the right platform, the reason for travel keeps changing, there is a vast net of relations to be negotiated among friendly strangers, arguments I do not understand, a web of mores, customs, timetables, and I can never place myself in order to either catch the train or settle down.

I book a ticket at the arts centre to see Laurel and Hardy, crab in the trousers, vertigo, and A Cottage on Dartmoor, its final shots of the dying hero's viewpoint turning into an unpeopled landscape.

So who watches?

The walk has shown me a landscape squaring up to death. The shapes of death – memento mori, gargoyles, morbid monsters, hunters, roadkill – have become

part of an orrery of the vitality of *things* rather than of organisms. Death is not an organising structure, ghosts are metaphors not monsters; death is fragmentation, real but eventual. Not an anaemic exchange of 'dust to dust', not a parody of commerce, not a balance, but a dispersal. Blue plaques for everyone! Swamp the culture of celebrity with ordinariness; fame for all!

During the *My Woman* sequence in a talkie cinema in the otherwise 'silent' *A Cottage On Dartmoor*, I think about three women, one I was stupid to leave, one I was right and lucky to stick with, and the third I loved-but-thankfully-mediated-the-feelings. The film deals rather well with loves: dark, pure, fire, blood.

In my room I work till 4am, work, work, read, read, write, write. Love it. Cannot relax because we die soon. Why bother to rest unless you have to?

I write about cities under the sea, Jules Verne, 'Stingray', Captain Nemo, gilled frogmen, mermen. Where does it come from, amphibian fantasy? Dagon. Innsmouth. The city beneath the sea becomes the coastal city impregnated by the depths, the coastal city becomes a beast that drags itself up from the depths and lies gasping on the coast, a city of id...

"There were no holy men. It was the places that were holy."

John Gaskin

A few highlights from other drifts and wanders (4)

ʰH On Offa's Dyke on a symbolic walk nearly 40 years ago, first waiting nervously for my turn to set off, one of three travellers. First refusing an apple offered, and then at a portal I was faced by Anna clutching a wooden post, a trickle of blood on her forehead, she launched the post at me and I blacked out and the next thing I remember I had the post in my arms and was further up the path, lying across which I found a man unable to walk and, putting the post over my shoulders, like a yolk, I supported him on my back and set off again along the path, to what he and I did not know...

ʰH On a rather dry local history orientated wander in Manchester, happening upon a young woman sat, legs akimbo, on the steps of a railway bridge applying palmfuls of fake tan to her legs (I was the only one impressed by this.)

ʰH On a 'body walk' through Munich, the sight of naked bathers moving between the rooms of the Volkbad, like souls in the ancient Egyptian afterlife; rather more impressive than my losing my way in the corridors to the changing rooms and stumbling naked into the café.

ʰH My first ever 'accidental' drift: walking the cold industrial wastelands of Stalowa Wola after refusing to get back in the theatre van after a crash.

ʰH Walking with digital image maker L.M.H.C. aka Leah in Holyhead, I drew chalk lines from the Raj Indian Restaurant and the Chinese takeaway next door across the road to the Empire Tanning Studio.

ʰH Being mobbed by two hundred over-enthusiastic Shanghai traders after drifting into their empty market, worried not for myself but for the safety of the traders, I escaped under a banner reading SMASHING SHEDS OF ILLEGAL MANAGEMENT (cracking down on the stalls of unlicensed traders), vaulted the market wall, and hid in a deserted dinosaur museum.

ʰH Gently persuading a doubtful concierge to let Bianca, John and me into some underground stables in Naples, to find they had been turned into a bouquet factory: the lithe hands of the men assembling the bouquets, the colours of the flowers in piles on the tables, the aromas!

And so many more.

> *"I predict the development of the 'Natural History of the Streets'....*
> *a study full of possibilities... Daily our streets are changing and the*
> *men and women who crowd them."*
> Geoffrey Murray, *The Gentle Art of Walking*, 1939

13.10.11

When I finally get to sleep it is only to fall into yet another anxiety dream: an exam in which I cannot write, while a charismatic teacher gives clues that I do not hear, surrounded by falling glitter, things in pieces, all make no sense... and although the dream goes on it is all coloured by my early failure... I throw the exam papers to the floor, then go back to retrieve them, but things have passed on, the exam is over... I am very relieved to wake up.

This is my sixteenth B&B. Nice bath. The owner explains that he has recently given up doing B&B and only took me on because my original booking fell before he closed down. I am staying in an unreal B&B, suspended between B&B and non-B&B.

The house is called Folly View, a reference to a gravel pit, next door, sixty foot deep, a speculative venture that failed, dug at the behest of a Mr Bird who lived in the neighbouring Castle House. After eating Folly View's final breakfast, I half-heartedly wander about in the town. Locate the faded advert for FROST, the retailer-ancestors of David Frost, the broadcaster. I look again at the strange animals on Thoroughfare: Reynard the Fox on the right? A fox with a basket, a monkey and a cat? Reynard the physician holds a basket of medicinal herbs, the hare (mistaken for a monkey, shape-shifting), his messenger, holds a flask. A sick lion, not a domestic cat, licking his wounds ... it should be dark red against a white background, but it looks carbonised, charred black. Lions either side of the heraldic shield. Ganymede holding a cup or glass, being seized by Jupiter in the form of an eagle, to be cup-bearer for the gods. The Lords of Halesworth until 1424 were cup-bearers at Royal coronations.

I hang about the local library adding scraps to the orrery, in danger of overweighting the whole thing and tipping it over. 1645, Halesworth's Sarah Spindler found to have three images like birds, two like moles, on her body: "employed them in several murders", hanged 27th of August. A "witch" at Dunwich, Elizabeth Southerne confessed to conversing with the Devil in the form of "a crabfish", he nipped her, fetched blood and they sealed a 14-year covenant, then the Devil "lay with her"; he was cold, but she did not see his shape. On another occasion he appeared as a "hairy black boy ten years old, who promised to give her 2s 6d, but did not".

On the day of the execution of Mother Lakeland in Ipswich, "a bunch of flesh, resembling the form of a dog, which grew upon the thigh of Mr Beale, and had hitherto proved impossible to remove, broke without any application of force, and a running sore commenced to heal."

Thomas and Mary Everard of Halesworth saw a "black dog like a water dog [that] made no noyse." A man felt something on his legs in bed, in the shape of a rabbit; it asked him if he would love it and deny God and Christ and he refused, but he agreed later when he met it in a field. The man was "switched" and told he now had teats from which imps would suck. I have had enough.

I walk to the station even though I have still an hour to wait. I contemplate the empty lager cans on the tracks, the used condom on the railway platform, the disused lavatories, their door kicked in to reveal something unpainted for decades.

I am on the train now; replaying parts of my route. We pass through Darsham, Wickham Market, Melton, Woodbridge. Two or three times I had crossed this track. I think of the roads, the wreck of a car in a fire station yard. I see the White House Farm at Darsham and the Londis where I shopped. The Halfway Café.

Sometimes on the Roman Road and around The Saints it felt as if I had slipped through unseen, by timing my walking so I kept hedges between me and residents in their lonely yards, even the dogs barked at a vague presence rather than at me; I had begun to fade there, a dark clad figure, just a shadow of some movement in the trees, changing from the shadowy devil-shaped-like-a-crabfish to the bright cellar, the Cave, dark on the outside, bright within.

I see a flurry of feathers from under the wheels of the train and pheasants take off across the fields. We are approaching Rendelsham Forest, more pheasants sent scattering by the train. What grabs me is not the arrangement of evidence, but the process of investigation and the small things 'to the side' of what is important, like the "bunch of flesh" this morning.

We are now at Wickham Market, where I had arrived just in time to catch my train to Darsham. What if the train were suddenly to turn and, on closed and buried tracks, take us all to Dunwich again?

There is the busy road into Woodbridge that I tramped. I cross my route yet again; my walk is unravelling, the film playing backwards, the spool spilling the images like gore onto a sloping floor.

The track now runs parallel to my route into Woodbridge. A scarecrow is supine in a garden, its arms bent and thrown out wide. I think of the abattoirs, the black dog on the bookmakers, the Russian doll-like Aggressors, the elf in the pork pie hat... and I slump back, happily exhausted into my seat, and the whole terrain lights up, a Cobra Mist covering a Suffolk landscape, its lighthouse UFOs winking their beams, transfiguring the white deer in the forest, the Herringfleet watchpost, the Martello towers, humming on a spiritual broadband, Sizewell C and a half hovering, the Vulcans swinging on their pub sign, the giant Toby Jug outside the Decoy Tavern shaking his fist of beer, the church of St Edmund's whirling, and all of them, lit up, spiralling round the philosopher's stone outside St Mary's. A personal cosmology to carry home; a free citizen among my own associations.

We pass the road I had stumbled down on sore blisters to ask at the TIC about the Rendelsham UFO Trail and was made to feel suitably odd and lonely. The slope up which the Angles dragged the funeral boat in which they buried their King, now eaten away to a stain. And finally we have left the route and begun the journey home.

At Ipswich I have a long delay before my next train, so I buy presents for Nikki, Rachel and Daniel and re-read some more of H. P. Lovecraft's *The Dunwich Horror*: "past, present, future, all are one in Yog-Sothoth. He knows where the Old Ones broke through of old, and where They shall break through again." Not far out of Ipswich I begin to fall asleep, walking to a place where nothing can be written about, from where nothing meaningful can be brought back.

On arriving home... well, I cannot now, almost two years after, recall what I did. I asked my partner, Nikki, and nor could she. "You are always going off and coming back; it's nothing special," she said. Abrupt returns to the everyday. On my return I did not collapse, but a few months later I returned with the filmmaker Siobhán Mckeown and sound recordist Chris Pepler to many of the places described here to make 'Tactics For Counter-Tourism: 31 short films'. The second part of my walk had been largely solo. I had intended to walk with more companions, but due to the postponement of my original timetable people were no longer free. I still wanted to share some of my adventures and it is testimony to Siobhán's openness and creativity that within and across the micro-films of 'Tactics For Counter-Tourism' is a hidden narrative of this walk and its spaces, including its esoteric bookcase, the raising of its sunken city and a visit to the museum of a thing that never happened.

The preparation of this book was interrupted for ten days of family holiday in the summer of 2013. We stayed at Lake Balaton in Hungary, on the southern shore, a working-class resort popular with Hungarians and Germans and a place where divided families would meet up during the Cold War. One day Tomasz suggested we take a trip and we visited a nature reserve and a museum site. After lunch, and black beer (no Soproni Demon available so I drank Arany Ászok's *felbarna*), my habitual restlessness kicked in and I left the three families exploring the indoor displays of the museum, fragments of stone rood screen rescued from buildings in numerous local villages, a stuffed and lacquered giant wels catfish behind blue David Lynch curtains, to sneak off around the back of the building.

Beyond the remnants of a brewery and the suspiciously even walls and tower stump – a few modern wooden stairs heading off into the blue sky – of a tenth-century church, I headed for an overgrown area which, according to the general map of the site, contained the surviving shapes of an earlier fortified religious complex. The people who had settled here lived hard, short lives, their bones marked with battle scars, an average age in the late 30s, religious warriors buried in fine jewellery. The one remaining element of their chapel is a spiral pillar, sharply contrasting with the grid of tiled flooring of its very recent 'reconstruction'.

In 38° of heat, I stumbled up a trodden dirt path between two large heaps of soil, expecting to wander around in undergrowth detecting something like the mounds of barrows, but instead what opened up was the taped and sharply spaded pit of an archaeological dig; human sized plastic coverings indicated that graves were open here.

No one was about; the dust and dryness everywhere suggested that the dig had been left for a while; perhaps for a summer break. Careful not to tread beyond the taped perimeter, I moved closer, struggling down the slopes of spoil, but soon found myself among piles of human bones and patterned pottery shards. I began to retreat quickly up the slithery spoil, but froze as on the far side of the excavated pit, some fifteen yards from where I stood, surely unaffected by me, part of the face of the excavation wall began to collapse in a rush of falling fragments and a cloud of dust. Absurd and frightening, too like a scene from *Quatermass and the Pit* to be taken seriously. Fear tunnelled my vision, the painful sun blurred things, the dust threw up a kind of Mist. I tried to focus on where the wall had collapsed, but it looked jelly-like, opaque...

The fire doors of perception

IN A FEW SECONDS YOU CAN TEACH yourself to look self-referentially.

Focus on a small detail, say, a light switch, on a wall a few metres away. Hold your focus on the detail; now what can you see in your field of vision? You should be able to pick out the edge of your nose. You may also notice that across your field of vision things are not all the same; at the edges the image is less distinct and distinctly curved.

Once you get the hang of this, you can call it up at any time; a way of placing yourself in all the images you see. Not in a world of high definition wrap-around narrative, but uneven and framed partiality.

By closely attending to your perceptions, you may begin to notice a certain folding dance of seeing. Watch how as you walk through a door or archway the world first closes in and then unfolds again. Passing through multiple portals or arches can be like a visual breathing. Enjoy how, as you reach the brow of a hill or turn a corner, you can literally fold in a new vista. Ask yourself: is there any politics woven into these narratives of perception? Any meaning to the sequences of wrappings up and unfoldings, to the rhythms, quick or drawn out, of the narrowings of focus and its opening up once more.

...with a sigh of tumbling dust the wall of earth began to collapse again and I backed further away.

In the first moment of looking, at the sound of the first fall, I thought I saw within the greyish brown of the dust, picked out in the fire of the sun, fragments of red, white and black, as if the earth for a moment showed its parts before withdrawing them.

I backed away in a panic; hardly able to see the ground under my feet, but certain that I had come to an end point here, a wall of unstable provenance. That, like the moment I stood by the 'druid's stone' and hesitated, I was not ready for this. That the chosen walking of this book had brought me here, but could take me no further and that to enter the spaces now on offer, to speak to what it is that speaks from within the stone and to look without fear on what crumbles from inside the earth, I would have to learn to walk in a different kind of space; the space of utter unpredictability.

In his film *The Great Walk*, writer and director Clive Austin describes seven dimensions of walking, of which the sixth is 'mythogeographic'. It is now time to risk making a complete fool of myself and attempt the seventh layer.

The last tactic

In my book *Mythogeography* I described and illustrated two grand structures of performance. For an example of the first, I borrowed a sketch drawn by the poet Basil Bunting to represent the structure of a Western classical symphony.

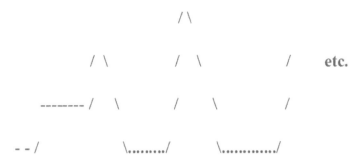

Bunting used this pattern of valleys and peaks, tension, delays, deferrals, releases, depressions and returns in the making of his long poem 'Briggflatts'; something I had the privilege of hearing him read shortly before his death. As an example of the second grand structure, I gave Kathakali dance-theatre and its quickly elevated and long-sustained heightened plane of consistency, maintaining without rising tension a massively extended climax stretching through the performance and out from it, a level of energy and pleasure remaining all the time as a kind of default around which the narrative action could weave over, under and around.

```
_____l_____ _ _ _ _ _ _ _
    /                                  l
    /                                  l
    /                                  l
    /                          (end of performance)
    /
```

In the walkings I propose and practise, the default pattern is always the second; a pattern that Gregory Bateson called a "continuing plateau of intensity", a strange stabilisation of self-sustaining heightened intensity that he observed in certain sexual games and quarrels on Bali; a plateau in place of climax or violence, in place of conclusion or crisis.

If I were to be autobiographical for a moment, I might connect this preference to an experience I had when I was about 10 or 11. It was at a party held one afternoon by a girl in her home next to the church. Her parents had, unusually, left us to it. There were about equal numbers of boys and girls, perhaps slightly more girls, about fifteen of us in total, all approximately the same age. The girls wanted to play 'spin the bottle' and I was the only boy there willing to join in, so I spent an afternoon kissing seven or eight girls. It was all very innocent and I felt no frustration that it went no further than kissing: it was a pleasure without conclusion that could go on forever. I do wonder whether it is that young joy that I still feel for the destinationless journey and its plane of dispersed ecstasy.

There is, of course, always a solo line of thoughts and physical tangents improvising around the pleasure plateau; sometimes quieter and less insistent than the heightened drone of the plateau, but moving up and down like the valleys and peaks of Bunting's model, and sometimes irrational and even shrieking and howling; its gentle abrasions and chaotic clawing are always threatening to raise the plateau up to the blue or drag it down into the bushes.

Where the plateau is serene, the solo line is necessarily obscene and inspired.

It is the great work of the great walk to reconcile these two walks; releasing and sustaining the poised inner fire from within the putrescent fragments of rot, ruin and revolutionary wreckage from which it comes in flesh and blood walking.

What the outcome of this wedding with the next road might be, I have no idea; for I am only one of the candidates for initiation in a rite that doesn't really exist yet, briefly appearing here in the avatar of my birth name, I hope I can now slip more effectively away to a new 'work' in unfamiliar spaces and under a new unconvincing aka, a little to the side of the Samsāra, just out of picture on the CCTV monitors...

> *"When you fall by the wayside, prop yourself up and be a menhir for the next walker."*

...and now it is time to walk...

Walk, focussing on a single cell in your body.

Now on all the cells, individually.

Bury something.

Walk for a day across a city collecting texts – edit them into a novella overnight – next day write the novella in graffiti across the city.

Build ruin.

Each day for a week take a different fast food for a walk.

Take something impossible.

Choose a large, accessible building and walk around it as if it were an 'art of memory', ascribing a different idea to each artefact and a different theory to each room. Once you have so treated the entire building, leave it. Don't return. Over time visit the building in your mind, allowing its ideas and theories to adapt and refurbish themselves as your memory of the building shifts and fades. If you ever lose interest in the ideas and theories, then return to the actual building and fill it with new ones, or sweep it clean ready for others to use.

Seek out fake ancientness – children's playground stone circles, parkland menhirs – and treat them as if they were the real thing.

Burn your maps. Scatter their ashes over the terrain they presume to represent..

If you have ever hurt another person in a public place, leave the person alone but make your apologies to the place.

Take a handful of dirt from the path and form the idol of your steps. For three minutes: worship. Then return the dust to the path.

For a year walk only when it rains.

Walk without money.

The day before, decide to walk. Dress appropriately. Go to sleep. Begin your walk the moment you wake.

Walk between properties that are colonial and colonised, robbed and rich, repressive and libidinous, queered and straitened, powerful and anti-power, fish and bait, public and private – draw lines of chalk to connect their opposites.

Walk the entire border of a copse, then a wood, then a forest. Stand at the mouths of footpaths and look in. Do not enter until you are invited.

Turn your left foot into a shrine.

Walk the green lanes. Walk the red roads. Walk the grey streets. Walk the orange alleys.

Walk with a grain of sand balanced on a fingertip.

Walk away from the end of the world.

Walk the shape of other people's love for you.

Take a shadow for a stroll.

Knock on the next door.

Go to the place that you feel weakest.

Walk away for a long while.

Appendix

Walking for a change: A manifesto for a new nomad

THERE IS NO SUCH THING AS A HUMAN BEING. At least, not in the way that there is such a thing as a mountain, or such a thing as a saucepan. Not because those things are unchanging; on the contrary, they all erode and rust and vibrantly erupt and change. But only the human being *chooses* to change (or stay the same as failingly best it can); indeed a human being is incapable of not choosing, though its choices may be fearfully restricted by oppressive regimes, violent partners, the promiscuity of gravity or global producers of passivity. Only in military marches is there no choice about which foot to step off with. And even in marches someone, somewhere must first choose between "by the left!" and "by the right!"

So, while psychoanalysts, gamblers and prophets may attempt to predict human futures on the basis of past behaviours, numbers, holy verses or material circumstances (and sciences have as much of a problem with this as religions) there is never any adequate fixed measure or template against which to lay the bets. Call it morphology or dynamic patterns, chaos theory or complexity, no matter how perceptive about the tidal turns or abrupt liquefactions, no one is ever quite sure of the extent of the field; or just how extended the extended organism really is. Economists can readily explain the last recession, but invariably fail to see the next one. Human nature – like free beer – is only ever available tomorrow. It is something that is always *going to be* made; an aspiration for which the sign is always already up and lit. Which is why utopias are only useful up until the moment that some bright sparks attempt to realise one. They are helpful and inspiring mirages, diaphanous signposts to what is not quite hidden far beyond them, but as blueprints they will soon become as bloodied as butchers' aprons.

A walk is a good model for this human existentialism.

A walk is nothing until it is over and then it is too late; which may explain the rarity of really good books about walking. The researcher in pursuit of lost gems will have plenty of topsoil to work through. For every Machen, Poe or Bradbury there is a lorry load of 'walking essays' about an ambulation that is "meant to be pleasant, even charming, and so no one ever gets lost and lives on grubs and rainwater in a trackless forest, has sex in a graveyard with a stranger, stumbles into a battle, or sees visions of another world". (Rebecca Solnit).

The walk to nowhere in particular, the destinationless wander, the urban exploration, trespass, getting lost, strolling perversely slowly or going *a zonzo* all in their way have something of the same defiance of the essential and the universal. More importantly, though, is not that such a walking somehow sums up, encapsulates or allegorises a 'human condition', but rather that there are so many modes of it that it defies even its own capacities to express other things; trips up on its own multiplicity. Not armfuls of diversity, but sprawling, tumbling, spilling splashes, splinters and streams that evade anyone or anything trying to sweep them up.

Practised with a little strong-headedness, canniness and tactical nous, such a fractious walking can be a limited freedom; not an escape from circumstances, but an escape inside circumstances. I never feel 'free' when walking, but I do feel that I am an agent.

Of course, some people do, and need to, run away. But this is about walking away in curves.

Is all this coming across as so many empty assertions? After all, what for me are the most consistently tedious modes of walking are the ones most practised: family strolls after lunch, rambles, errands to the shops, pseudo-treks for subsequent publication, Macmillan Ways and Coastal Paths, walking the dog... and yet even these can be disrupted for a few moments by the myriad of other, non-functional modes: lyrical walking, art crawling, pilgrimage, and so on. During my recent evacuation across central Manhattan at walking pace in an NYPD van, courtesy of Frankenstorm Sandy, at times in fear for the lives of my partner and children, I was still able to make the best of the experience as a kind of extreme guided tour, enjoying the trees in Central Park seething in the darkness, the neon of Broadway bleeding in the rain down the van windows, a metal roadside sign flapping like a deranged clown, the van rocked by the winds like a ride in a cheap fairground simulator.

O, and by the way (for this is all "by the way"), that "and so on" in the middle of the last paragraph is what this is about, that "and so on" is agency; whether it is an agency that is already out there for you to take, enter, embrace, the intensity of one thing after another, the linear quest with its many branches – the yes or no of the junction – that strange feeling of authenticity on the road, a band of temporary friends together briefly, the mysterious stranger coming into town, the chameleon switching roles, the melting into the shadows that is a kind of everything... I don't know...

For that "and so on" is part of *A Plan*: a grand confluence of so many walkings that together will effect some qualitative shift at an unanticipated level... *A Plan* for unplannable things, the throw of the six thousand-sided die... *A Plan* whose beauty I hope you will acknowledge and then ignore.

The liberal and progressive 'new urbanist' ideals – of neighbourhood centres, easy but contained pedestrianism, mixed-use centres, designs for a Jane Jacobs city – are of no greater interest to this walking than the urban deserts of freeways and malls. That is not to say I do not think they are worth trying, but just that this is a less sociable walk than that; that given our spectacular circumstances, this walking can never be fully on the surface, can never quite trust the monster that lurks behind benevolence. Rather than seeking the mitigation of contradictions, this walking wants and needs gaps and fractures to make its way, tensions to serve as its capital and catapults, waste and ruins for its building materials.

This is not about final moves, but about positional shifts; the Long Revolution of satellite captures and asymmetrical actions, the regressing to simple memes in order to change ideological machines.

So, maybe I'll see you one day, out there, among the voids that work as decompression chambers, in the wastelands where interiority is possible again, in those excessive spaces that work like generators. And if not me, then, perhaps better, one of the ghosts that feed off me.

References

Boym, Svetlana (2008), *Architecture of the Off-Modern*. Buell Center/ FORuM Project and Princeton Architectural Press.

Debord, Guy (1994), *The Society of the Spectacle*. (Translated from French by David Nicholson-Smith.) Zone Books.

Heddon, Deidre & Turner, Cathy (2012), 'Walking Women: Shifting the Tales and Scales of Mobility', *Contemporary Theatre Review*, 22:2 224-236.

Heazell, Paddy (2010), *Most Secret: The Hidden History of Orford Ness*. The History Press.

Hewitt, Andrew (2005), *Social Choreography: Ideology as Performance in Dance and Everyday Movement*. Duke University Press.

Holliday, Robert Cortes (1918), *Walking Stick Papers*. George H. Doran Company.

Ingold, Tim (2011), *Being Alive*. Routledge.

Papadimitriou, Nick (2012), *Scarp*. Sceptre.

Reeve, Sandra (2011), *Nine Ways of Seeing a Body*. Triarchy Press.

Richardson, Tina (2012), *Concretes, Crows and Calluses: dispatches from a contemporary psychogeographer*. Particulations Press.

Suzuki, Tadashi (1986), *The Way of Acting*. (trans J. T. Rimer.) Theatre Communications Group.

Turner, Cathy (2001), 'Out of Place: The Politics of Site-Specific Performance in Contested Space' (a performance presentation).

Turner, J. Scott (2002), *The Extended Organism: The Physiology of Animal Built Structures*. Harvard University Press.

Williams, Evan Calder (2011), *Combined and Uneven Apocalypse*. Zero Books.

Dedication

This book is dedicated to all the exemplary walkers:
William Pope L. crawling up Broadway, Mahatma Ghandi marching for the right to gather salt, Carmen Papalia with his marching band mobility device, Kinga Araya in iron shoes, Blake Morris walking to thirty different homes and living in each for three days in NYC, Monique Besten walking and stitching, Tina Richardson whose schizo-cartography manifests the truth that psychogeographic walking only lives on when it is reworked in one's own shifting image, Helen Billinghurst getting out of her car and walking into a landscape she had driven past for twenty years, Jooyoung Lee walking convivially, Iain Sinclair cutting a V through London, Ali Pretty and Richard White walking Wiltshire's white horses, Satish Kumar peace walking to Moscow during the Cold War, Dee Heddon walking one square foot, Mike Pearson for his tour of his childhood village, Francis Alÿs walking in magnets, my colleagues in Wrights & Sites for never walking the same road twice and putting up with me, Roy Bayfield walking to the anomalous Google Maps town of Argleton, Hamish Fulton hallucinating on the Pilgrim's Way and choreographing a walk for locals in Huntly, Stephen Graham zig-zagging, Barry Patterson for dialoguing with the genius loci, Rev. John Davies walking the M62, Amy Sharrocks falling, Charles Hurst acorn planting, Shea Craig the walking machine, Townley and Bradby for walking with a half-brick…. you know who you are!!

> *"Only the person for whom the whole world is like a foreign country is perfect."* St Victor of Hugo

Acknowledgements

I am responsible for all the images and illustrations in the book except for the following, for which I gratefully acknowledge their takers, creators, finders and contributors:

p. 7   Photograph by Mike Tooby.

p. 157   The photograph of the postcard of Henry Bensley is in the public domain.

p. 162   The photograph of Amy Cutler as a zombie was contributed by Amy Cutler.

p. 184   Photograph by Ian Hughes.

p. 189   Photograph by Bryony Henderson.

p. 195   The painting, entitled The Long Walk, and the photograph of it, are by Helen Billinghurst. helenbillinghurst.blogspot.co.uk

p. 197   Photograph of the author by Rachel Sved.

Cover   The photograph of the pedestrian with its head in a drain is by Clive Austin, who also made The Great Walk, which is mentioned in several places in this book. facebook.com/TheGreatWalk

Cover   The photograph of the female pedestrian was taken and contributed by Photography and 3D Artist, Richard Jeffery. www.richardjeffery.com

Cover   The photograph of the parent and child pedestrians was taken and contributed by Performance Artist, Ignacio Pérez Pérez. facebook com/ignacioperezperez

About the Author

Dr Phil Smith is a prolific writer, performer, urban mis-guide, dramaturg (for TNT Munich), counter-tourist, drifter, artist-researcher and academic.

He has written or co-written over one hundred professionally produced works for a wide range of British and international theatres and touring companies, and has created and performed in numerous site-specific theatre projects, often with Exeter-based Wrights & Sites, of which he is a core member (www.mis-guide.com).

He is Associate Professor in the School of Humanities and Performing Arts at Plymouth University.

Phil has published papers in *Studies In Theatre and Performance, Cultural Geographies, Performance Research, Research in Drama Education* and *New Theatre Quarterly*, co-authored a range of Mis-Guides with the other members of Wrights & Sites and written or co-written several other books including: *Mythogeography: A Guide to Walking Sideways; Counter-Tourism: The Handbook; Counter-Tourism: A Pocketbook; A Sardine Street Box of Tricks* (all Triarchy Press) and *Walking, Writing and Performance* (Intellect, 2009).

See **www.triarchypress.net/crabman** for more information.

"Walking with Phil is like having my very own Dr Who."
Siobhán Mckeown, film maker and dj Shibby Shitegeist.

Lightning Source UK Ltd.
Milton Keynes UK
UKOW07f0509011114

240936UK00011B/130/P